HOME MADE
· WINE ·

·A·STEP·BY·STEP·
Guide to Making
HOME MADE
WINE

—Judith Irwin—

in conjunction with Roy Ekins

Bramley Books

Photography
Neil Sutherland

Design
Stonecastle Graphics Ltd

The publishers would like to thank all
those involved in the production of this
book, particularly Roz McCall of The
Home Liquor Company, Cranleigh,
Surrey, for her help and the loan of
equipment, Ann Harris and Bert Mower
for their help and advice, and
Brewmaker Ltd of Northam,
Southampton, for supplying equipment.

3136
This edition published in 1997 by
Bramley Books
© 1991 CLB International,
Godalming, Surrey
Printed and bound in Singapore
ISBN 1-85833-718-6

Preface

More and more people are taking up the pleasurable and creative pursuit of making their own wines, discovering in the process not just an absorbing hobby but also a network of enthusiasts just waiting to welcome the beginner into their midst. Throughout the country there are wine circles where individuals can get together to discuss recipes, swap tips and taste the fruits of each other's labours. What might seem at first glance to be a very private, even lonely, hobby can turn out to be just the opposite. There is also the attraction of possibly winning a prize for one's efforts at a show, to enhance the simple satisfaction of producing one's own wines. Whatever the reason for beginning, the rewards are many.

For me, home winemaking started as a hobby that has since completely changed my life, opening up a superb social life and giving me the opportunity to meet many people with the same interests. My hobby has also enabled me to travel around the country to various shows as a wine judge and to experience for myself the degree of devotion to the home production of wine that exists in some areas. Most important of all, through my hobby I have met some wonderful people and made some very good friends. I hope to pass on some of this enthusiasm and enjoyment to the beginner through *A Step-by-Step Guide to Making Home-Made Wine*.

I would like to dedicate the book to my father, William John Turner, whose love and understanding were always with me, and who introduced me to the hobby of winemaking.

Judith.

Contents

Chapter 1. WHAT IS WINE?

What is wine? Before you can make it, you must understand what it is, and why each of the different stages you go through contributes towards creating the whole. The Oxford Dictionary tells us that 'wine is the fermented juice of the grape' and that the word comes from the Latin vinum. If, however, you read further, or consult a winemakers' dictionary, a very different picture emerges. Here we learn that homemade wine is a liquid containing alcohol caused by natural fermentation. Fermentation is the process of yeast turning sugar into ethyl alcohol and carbon dioxide. This 'wine' can be made from any suitable fruit or vegetable juice with the addition of sugar, yeast, and various additives, which will be described in a later chapter.

Wine has been made for centuries in farmhouse kitchens using open earthenware crocks covered with cloths. The yeast in the early days was not the sophisticated product we know today, but was almost certainly the baker's variety used for making bread. This yeast was spread onto a slice of toast which was then floated on the top of the liquid in the crock. This method of production often allowed bacterial infection to spoil the wine. In some cases, potato wine being a good example, a certain amount of methyl alcohol was produced as well as the required ethyl alcohol. This, when taken in large quantities, can cause blindness and was one of the main reasons for the poor image homemade wine once had. It caused heavy drunkenness with even heavier hangovers and headaches the following day. The other reason that kitchen brews became figures of ridicule is that, as previously mentioned, the yeast turns the sugar into alcohol. It was therefore assumed that the more sugar used the higher the alcohol content the wine would have. We now know that all yeasts have a saturation point above which the alcohol level kills them, and any excess remaining sugar will result in an over-sweet wine. It was through problems like these that homemade wines became known as over- sweet, over-strong, and sometimes dangerous drinks.

This book shows, through text and pictures, how far we have travelled since those days. We can now produce well-made, well-balanced wines for any occasion, all without spending a vast amount of money on ingredients. It is quite possible to grow your own produce or to harvest the fruits of the hedgerows, and recipes using the best fruits and vegetables are all included here. **However, not all plants are suitable for winemaking and a general, though not exhaustive, list of poisonous or unsuitable plants is included on page 152. Readers are advised to consult this before experimenting.**

The advantages and disadvantages of winemaking.

The advantages of making your own wine have changed over the last few years. In the past a bottle of wine was a relatively expensive item, so it was only purchased for special occasions. These days a bottle of wine is within the means of most of us, which enables us to drink more often and to be more choosy. The other major factor is that it is now easy to purchase wine when doing the weekly supermarket shop. We are thus looking for very different reasons for becoming home winemakers, and for many the main one is challenge and fulfilment.

Take the autumn season as an example. You feel like going out for a Sunday afternoon walk with the family. With very little organisation it is possible to go out equipped with buckets or gathering utensils and arrive at an area where you will be able to pick blackberries. Four pounds is all you need to make a gallon of wine, and these are easily picked in an afternoon. After you have taken them home and processed them into six bottles of good, drinkable wine, imagine the feeling of pride when you offer your friends a glass of your own 'brew'.

If you are a keen gardener and like to grow your own vegetables, there can be even more of a challenge. Produce enough carrots to make a gallon, scrub and slice them and boil them in water until soft. Strain, and use only the water, or as we call it, 'gravy', to make the wine and then use or freeze the solids as a vegetable. Do make sure, however, that you do not salt them until the gravy has been taken off.

Finance still plays an important part as it is cheaper to make your own wine than to buy it. If you are growing or picking your ingredients they are obviously free to you. The only expense in this case is the sugar and the additives such as yeast and nutrients, which cost very little. If you are buying the fruits, such as peaches or apricots, this will obviously increase the basic cost. Bear in mind that it is not worth trying to save money by using inferior goods. Whatever is put into the wine will be reflected in the end product. In other words, if you use bruised or over-ripe fruit, those off-flavours will almost certainly be obvious in the taste of the finished wine. The one exception to this is the banana, which needs to be over ripe (black) to be at its best, because it is only in this state that it contains the required sugar.

One of the most important aspects of the hobby is the social side. Around thirty-five years ago a group of people living in the Andover area, all interested in making their own wines, decided to form a club and called it a Wine Circle. Since then there have been several hundred such wine clubs formed all over the country. Usually the meetings take place once a month and members go along, with one or two of their bottles of wine, to chat amongst themselves or to listen to an invited speaker. During the evening it is usual to taste and discuss your wines with friends or perhaps a visiting wine judge.

Another type of group which winemakers have organised is the Diners' Group, in which members, who all enjoy good wine with good food, take it in turns to entertain each other. To be able to find in your 'cellar' the different wines needed to accompany a full meal is not easy. You are likely to need an aperitif, a white and a red table wine, a dessert style wine, and even a liqueur. Anybody who has managed this successfully experiences a very great feeling of satisfaction.

Then there are the shows at which wine makers can compete against each other. These shows vary greatly in size, from the small wine sections in a horticultural show with perhaps a dozen bottles, to the National Association's annual show at which 5,000 or more bottles are displayed. To win a certificate, class or cup, or to become the Master Winemaker, all have their rewards and all start with a demijohn at home.

Wine making does, of course, have its problems. An amount of space is required in which to store the wine in the jars. To begin with this space has to be in the warm and at a constant temperature; perhaps by a radiator, on a specifically designed tray, or even in the airing cupboard. The use of the kitchen is also necessary, and difficulties can arise when the winemaking interferes with the cooking of the Sunday lunch.

One frustrating aspect is the time which must elapse between starting a gallon and when it becomes drinkable. Unfortunately, most people become impatient, and wine is often drunk before it is really ready. On the subject of timetables, it is worth making sure that you, or another reliable person, is going to be around when the next stage in any winemaking occurs. For instance, if a wine is due to be racked and you are going to be away for a fortnight, it can spoil by being left 'sitting' on the lees for too long. A last word of warning: be careful not to get too carried away. One gallon can soon multiply into ten, and then twenty, as enthusiasm grows, and all the above problems multiply with them.

Winemaking Equipment

Basic Equipment Required

It is not necessary to spend a great deal of money on equipment in the early stages of winemaking. Simply buy the basic essentials. For example, let us take the blackberry recipe which can be found in the 'autumn' section.

Possibly the first and most important factor to consider when making wine is cleanliness. It is absolutely essential that all equipment used is kept sterile. This is not difficult to do as sterilising agents are available in different forms, powder or tablet, under the trade name 'Campden tablets'. Providing you follow the easy directions your wine will not become infected by bacterial action.

When you have collected the ingredients together place them in a new **white plastic bucket**. Make sure that this will hold at least two gallons (nine litres) and has a tightly fitting lid. The important feature is that it is white, as any other colour can be affected by the alcohol, which may draw the poisonous colouring agent out and absorb it into the wine.

Pour onto the fruit four pints of boiling water; it is really advisable to boil all the water you are going to use. This eliminates the risk of off-flavours in the finished wine that could be caused by chemicals in the water. The fruit and liquids now in the bucket are known as the 'must'. Activate the yeast by adding it to a small amount of warm water, adding some sugar and leaving it in a warm place to start working. There are many different types of yeast available.

Leave for four days, stirring daily. The **spoon** should also be white plastic. If a wooden spoon is used there is a risk of bacterial infection. This is because the lip of a wooden spoon softens and cracks in hot water and bacteria can enter. The use of a metal spoon is not advisable as a chemical reaction can set up when metal is in contact with the acids and yeasts in the must.

Strain the must through a **sieve** or **nylon bag** into another bucket. There are several different, inexpensive straining bags on the market. You can also buy a white plastic funnel which has a sieve half way down. The sieve is removable for easy cleaning, and also to convert the funnel into a standard item. If neither of these methods are available you can use an ordinary piece of cheesecloth which is tied around the top of the second bucket. If another bucket is not available any vessel which can hold a gallon will do.

Pour the juice into a sterile **demijohn** and fit a bored **cork** or **rubber bung** and an **air lock**. These are items which must be purchased and are available from any shop selling home brew equipment.

Rack into another demijohn, again any vessel which can hold one gallon of liquid will do. The wine can always be poured back into the cleaned jar. In order to rack you need to buy a length of tubing, which can have a tap in the middle to enable you to stop and start the flow of the liquid. When you rack you must place the full jar on a higher level than the empty one. Then, by suction at the lower end of the pipe, start the wine flowing. Once started the liquid will continue to run

by gravity. Take care not to disturb the sediment at the bottom of the jar. Always make sure to top up the level in the clean jar to the shoulder, either with boiled water, fruit juice or another wine.

When finished close the jar with a **cork** or **safety closure**. It is very important that no air creeps into the vessel while the wine is maturing. Closures are available at any suitable shop. When the wine is ready you will need six bottles. These can be bought or collected in readiness. It is quite easy to soak off commercial labels and polish bottles. As already mentioned, cleanliness is all- important and this is very true where corks are concerned. It is preferable to buy new ones, as once a corkscrew has been used on a corks it is not reusable. The flanged style of cork is the best for the beginner, as they can be used again provided they are sterilised.

(1) *A sterile demijohn;* **(2)** *one type of bored bung and airlock;* **(3)** *a demijohn fitted with a siphon;* **(4)** *a selection of hydrometers and a trial jar;* **(5)** *a thermal belt and* **(6)** *an immersion heater – both aid fermentation in cold or fluctuating temperatures.*

1

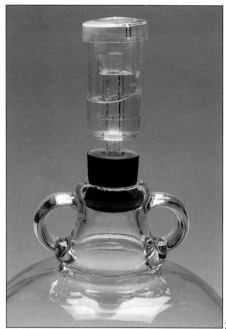

2

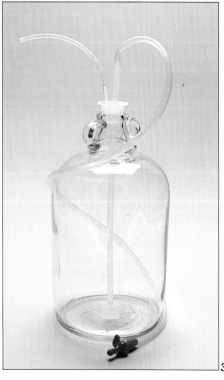

3

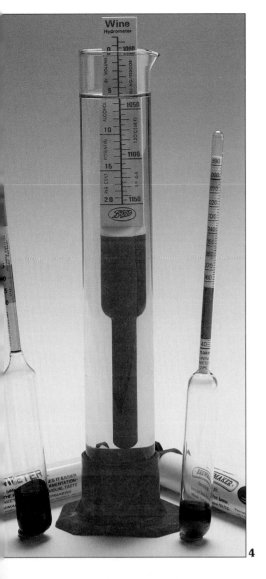

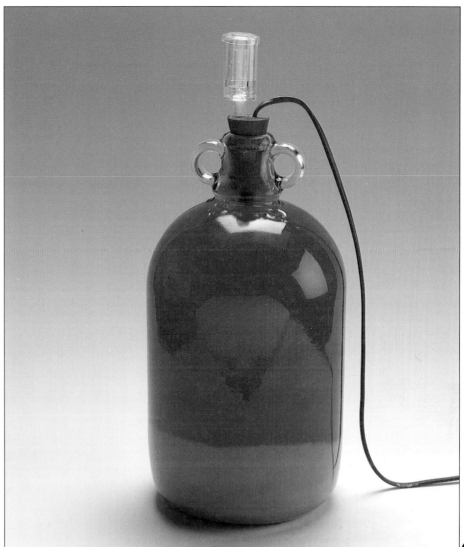

More sophisticated equipment

After you have made your initial beginners' gallon you will very soon want to be more adventurous. Spend some time studying the stock available at your local shop. The choice will be considerable, and you will certainly wish to try out some of the winemaking aids. One really helpful aid is some method of keeping the fermenting must at a constant temperature. There is a heat tray which comes in three sizes, to hold one, two, or four demijohns. These use mains electricity, but consume very little power. There is also an electrically heated belt which wraps around the jar and a rod which fits into the liquid through the neck of the demijohn.

To control the level of acid in the wine is also very important, and there are several means of checking it. Possibly the most accurate is the titration kit. This is a kit which contains the chemicals needed to assess the level of acid in the wine. It comes complete with full instructions. An easier, if not so accurate, way is the Rapitest. This is a small dial with an attached probe which goes into the wine, and again full instructions come with the package.

There are several different racking tubes, all of which have their advantages. One has a glass tube which goes into the jar. This is finished off with a 'U' bend which reduces the risk of disturbing the sediment. Another has a second, small tube lying alongside the main one, which acts to draw off the air and stop the flow when a demijohn is full. This is especially useful when racking from a five gallon container into separate jars. All racking tubes work by gravity.

(1) *A thermal demijohn cover aids fermentation in cold or fluctuating temperatures.* (2) *Equipment for bottling, corking, naming, recording and storing the finished wines.* (3) *White plastic fermentation buckets and a long thermometer.*

   Airlocks come in all shapes; some made in glass and some in plastic. They all fit into corks or rubber bungs which have a hole bored through them. If you are short of storage space it is worth looking around, as some airlocks are much taller than others. The corks fit either one gallon or five gallon jars and can be made from the traditional cork or rubber. If the rubber ones are used it is advisable to wrap them in cling film if using the jar for storage, or the wine can take on the taste of oxidising rubber. The bung may also in time weld itself to the jar. It is a good idea to use a coloured liquid in the airlock, so you can see at a glance if it is dry or not.

   Presentation of the finished, bottled product is important. It is possible to buy a whole range of labels, or you can design your own. The field for this is unlimited; you can name the wine after either the ingredient or style (e.g. Sweet Rosehip and Fig, or Cream Sherry-Style etc.). If you are designing your own, you can invent a trade name, e.g. 'Vin de Maison' or 'Chateau Clarke'. If you do not wish to use a flanged cork it is easy, with a corker, to use long, cylindrical corks. To enhance these there are capsules of different colours. These are either plastic, which shrink to fit the bottle neck when in contact with hot water, or gold or silver foil. All add to the appearance of the finished product.

Equipment for showing wine.

The only additional equipment needed is the show bottles and corks. The bottles have to hold 75cl and be of clear glass. As it is very difficult to obtain completely clear glass today, a tint of pale green is now accepted. The bottles must have a punt in the base and be of the 'claret bottle' shape. The corks are flanged style and vary in colour according to the show. Recently, most show organisers have adopted the white, plastic-topped kind. No markings of any sort are allowed on the bottle except the official label, which is provided at the time of entry.

(4) Assorted airlocks and bored bungs. (5) Funnels, a straining bag, a sieve and a long-handled white plastic spoon are some of the additional items of equipment that may be required. (6) Filtering and the addition of fining agents ensures crystal-clear wines for showing.

5

2

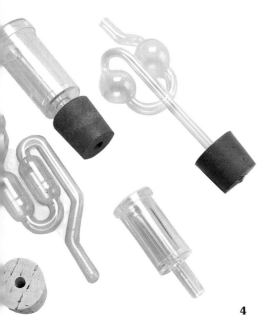

4

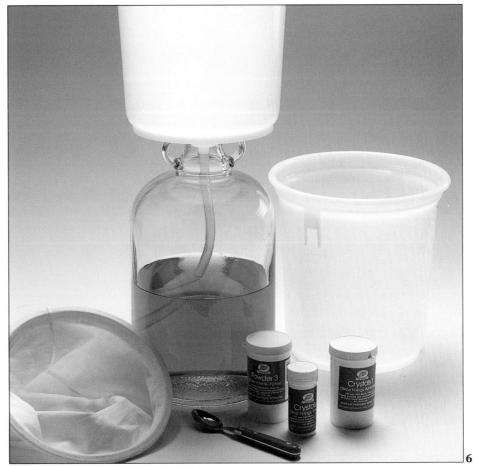

6

Yeast and Fermentation

The methods of using yeast and the types employed have varied greatly since wine production began. The Romans are known to have made wine from natural ingredients, and this included wild yeast. Grapes when picked have a noticeable 'bloom' on their skins, and this is a wild yeast. The disadvantages of allowing this to become active is that not only are wild yeasts present but also other bacteria and fungi, not noticeable to the eye. For this reason we wash and sterilise our ingredients, and in doing so kill such living organisms, including the wild yeast. The use of baker's yeast was the next method of introducing it. This was spread thinly on a slice of toast which was floated on top of the fermentation vessel. This had drawbacks, as the wine often had a 'bready' flavour, and it was left uncovered and exposed to any infection around.

With the growth of interest in making wine at home various new types of yeast appeared on the market. Firstly an all-purpose type was introduced which was suitable to use when making any style of wine. This is still available and is very good, especially if you are just beginning the hobby. Next came the different types for the different styles of wine, for example when making a dry white wine you use a sachet of yeast suitable for dry white wine. Even more sophisticated are the sachets for particular wines, for example a 'Chablis' yeast for making a 'Chablis style' wine. There are companies which specialise in various yeasts and they have introduced liquid cultured varieties. These are very refined, and a tremendous amount of research has gone into producing them.

It is the yeast that turns the sugar in the must into the alcohol required. It actually produces fifty per cent carbon dioxide and fifty per cent alcohol. It is the carbon dioxide which we see as bubbles coming through the air lock. In order to do its job the yeast needs a constant temperature of between 19-21°C (66-70°F). If it is too hot the yeast cells will die, and if it is too cold the rate of growth is slowed right down.

There are two different kinds of fermentation, the aerobic and the anaerobic. The first, aerobic, is with oxygen. This produces a very fast fermentation while in the bucket or vessel. There is not much alcohol produced and it should only last for a few days. The second, anaerobic, is without oxygen. This takes place in the demijohn under an airlock. It is much slower, and can last for a long time. Most of the alcohol is produced at this stage.

The yeast cells reproduce themselves at a very fast rate, several thousand per hour. When these cells are spent they fall to the bottom of the jar and form a sediment. If the wine is left on these dead cells for any length of time an off flavour can be picked up. The yeast cells will usually be killed by the alcohol when it reaches 15-16 per cent by volume; it is therefore almost impossible to produce a wine with a higher alcohol content unless by the addition of spirit.

Nutrients and Acids.

Most recipes quote the various additives to use but it is important to know why they are being used. If, as you become more confident, you wish to invent recipes, it is also important to know what other ingredients may be necessary.

Yeast Nutrient. As its name implies, this helps to feed and encourage the yeast. It is commonly a mixture of ammonium sulphate and ammonium phosphate. The easiest way of acquiring this is to purchase one of the well known brands on sale in the homebrew shops, although it is possible to produce your own by buying the chemicals and blending them. One teaspoon is generally sufficient. The Vitamin 'B' is also an aid to the yeast and this can be purchased in small (3mg) tablet form. The addition of one of these tablets per gallon is enough in most cases, but in a flower or vegetable must two tablets are advisable.

Acids. The grape contains all the natural acids required to produce wine. We do not have that advantage with the ingredients we use, so must add them. We do this not only for the taste – the wine would be completely bland without acids – but to help keep the yeast alive. There are three major acids used: citric, malic, and tartaric. At one time only citric acid was used, and it was added in the form of lemons or oranges. This is not really a reliable guide as the size of the fruits varies, so we now use a powdered form. Usually one teaspoon is sufficient, but this depends on the main ingredient of the wine. If this has a high acid content, use less than a teaspoon; if it is very low, as with flowers, use more.

The other two acids are also available in powder form and some people like to use a mixture of all three. Tartaric acid has one distinct advantage over the others in that if there is a surplus in the finished wine, this will crystallize out if the wine is kept at a low temperature.

Other Additives.

Tannin. The grape provides an adequate supply of this necessary ingredient. It is contained in the skin and is extracted at the same time as the colour pigment. When we make red wine from natural fruits, such as elderberries or blackberries, we do not need to add tannin. There is more than enough put there by nature, again in the skins. In fact we have to be very careful not to extract more than we need. For this reason it advisable not to ferment the fruit pulp for too long.

When making white wine or wine from such ingredients as flowers tannin must be added. Any of the manufactured products on the market can be used. It is still also possible to use, as our forefathers did, cold tea, as the same tannin is contained in wine as in tea.

It good to remember that the more tannin a wine contains, the longer that wine needs to be matured before it can be drunk.

Pectin enzyme. One problem that does arise when making our own wines is the presence of hazes. However fine a wine's bouquet and taste, if it is not perfectly clear it is not fully appealing. These hazes are caused by jelly-like substances (pectins) which are present in the juices. They are increased if very hot or boiling water comes into contact with the juice. To avoid the risk of this problem we add a pectin destroying agent. This is a completely harmless addition, a natural enzyme, and modern practice is to add it to all musts that contain fruit. As a matter of interest it is the pectin present in fruit which causes the 'set' in jam making when a certain temperature is reached.

Campden tablets. As already mentioned, Campden tablets can be used as a sterilising agent. This is not, however, their only use. They are a solid form of sodium metabisulphite, which can be used to inhibit the growth of the yeast. They can also be used to sterilise and clean the fresh ingredients before fermentation. Because these two functions are somewhat contrary, care must be

(1) A bucket of freshly harvested grapes. **(2)** The natural, waxy bloom on a grape contains the fruit's yeast reserves. It is these yeasts that attack the sugar in the grape juice during fermentation, turning it into alcohol.

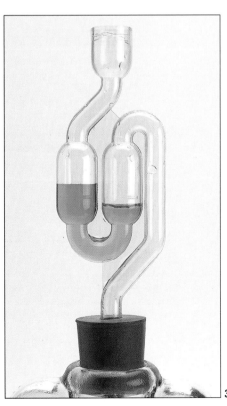

(3) & **(4)** *As fermentation progresses carbon dioxide is forced through the air lock. The cotton wool prevents impurities entering the air lock.*

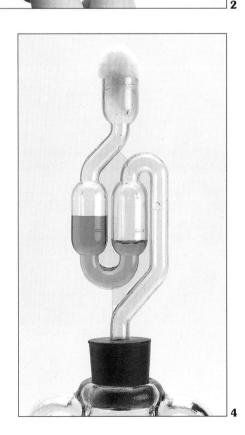

taken not to over-sulphite the initial must, otherwise the yeast will not be able to start fermenting. The maximum amount that is safe to use is two crushed tablets per gallon, and use them at least 24 hours before you add the yeast.

Because the tablets will inhibit the growth of the yeast they are also used when the wine is finished. When the wine is racked (the sediment syphoned off), the addition of one crushed tablet will greatly decrease the risk of re-fermentation, and prevent oxidation of the wine. There are, as always, some disadvantages, and the main one is that the presence of sodium metabisulphite in wine is noticeable both in the taste and the bouquet. With time both of these characteristics will fade, but it is not advisable to add too much. One crushed tablet at the first and last rackings is sufficient, it is not necessary to add one to any intermediate racking.

Sugar in Wine. After the yeast, this is the most important addition to the wine. No sugar – no alcohol – no wine! Too little sugar will result in too low an alcohol level and therefore an unbalanced wine. Too much sugar and the wine will end up as an over-sweet drink. If this happens there is no way of reducing the sugar level unless you blend it with a very dry wine.

Yeast turns the sugar, which is in the form of sucrose, into glucose and fructose. The technical name for this is invert sugar; it can be bought but is rather expensive. The advantage of this invert sugar is that the fermentation starts more quickly. We can help the yeast by making a syrup. Sugar, in the form we know it, is dry and heavy. If you place it, as it is, into the demijohn it will fall to the bottom and become a solid mass. It is advisable, therefore, to turn it into sugar syrup. To do this you place two pounds of sugar into one pint of water and bring it to the boil, stirring frequently. This will produce two pints of syrup can be used more easily.

3

1

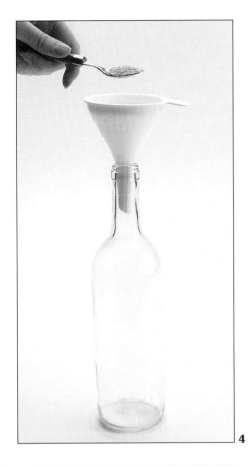

4

5

6

2

7

Yeast should always be activated before being added to the must. (3) Put the sugar in the starter bottle, (4) add the yeast and (5) the water as directed. (6) Stop the bottle with cotton wool and (7) wait for fermentation to begin.

(1) Part of the syphoning process. (2) Using a heating tray to aid fermentation.

Yeast can only handle a certain amount of sugar at one time. Because of this, if you are attempting to make a dessert style wine, which needs a high alcohol level, it is advisable not to use all the sugar at once. After the initial two pounds has resulted in an early, fast fermentation, the rest can be added, in the form of sugar syrup, daily in two ounce measures. In order to calculate the amount of sugar needed for the required alcohol, a general rule is that two pounds of sugar will produce nine to ten per cent alcohol by volume, but there are other things to take into consideration. These will be explained in detail later.

Different types of sugar can be used for different wines. Generally we use ordinary granulated white sugar, as this does not have any strong flavour. If, however, you want to make, say, a Madeira style wine, you can use a dark brown sugar. If when the wine is finished you wish to sweeten it slightly you can buy non-fermentable sweeteners, which have obvious advantages. Honey can also be used as a sweetener, but does have a very distinctive flavour, and can cause re-fermentation. Wine made using only honey is called Mead.

The Hydrometer, or Saccharometer

It is a basic fact that wine is not wine unless it contains alcohol. The amount of alcohol in wine is a very important factor, and one that we can control. Yeast turns the sugar into roughly 50 per cent carbon dioxide and 50 per cent alcohol, so how much sugar we add determines how much alcohol we finish with. There are, of course, other factors involved in deciding this. If all the sugar is not converted we will be left with an over-sweet wine with insufficient alcohol. For this reason we have already discussed the temperature needed to encourage the yeast's growth.

The amount of alcohol needed for different styles of wine varies depending on the amount of body required and strength sought. The one common factor in all winemaking is **balance** and in this the alcohol level plays an important part. It is no longer necessary to guess the amount of sugar required to balance a wine as there are specific instruments available which, with very little practice, will enable you to calculate correctly the sugar needed to gain the alcohol required. These are called Hydrometers or Saccharometers.

The Hydrometer is a sealed glass or plastic tube, weighted at the base, with a graduated table down its stem. This table is marked in equal parts with corresponding numbers. The hydrometer is used in conjunction with a glass or plastic trial jar which can accommodate its length and allow the tube to float. To understand the readings you must follow the principle of the instrument. If you take water as a guide, a hydrometer floated in it will give a reading of 1000 at surface level at 59°F (15°C). If sugar is then dissolved in it, the water will become heavier, or denser, and the tube will not sink so far into it. If the scale is marked in divisions of ten, the reading could now be 1040, for example. From this you can see that the liquid has a specific gravity of 40. If, however, as in the case of wine, that sugar is fermented out, the liquid will become lighter than water due to its alcohol content, and the tube will sink further into the jar, and the reading could be 990. The scale has to be read at eye level for an accuracy and it is the point where the wine surface lies level that gives the correct reading. Do not take the reading at the edge, where the rim of the liquid (the meniscus) creeps up the side of the hydrometer.

Now to work out how this can help to achieve the amount of alcohol required. Almost all ingredients contain some sugar, and it is important that this sweetness is taken into consideration. If a hydrometer is used when the initial must is prepared, some of the liquid without any solids can be tested in the trial jar. A gallon of must containing two pounds of sugar will give an initial hydrometer reading of 1077. If the sugar is completely turned into alcohol, it will produce ten per cent alcohol by volume, and give a reading of 1000 or less on the hydrometer scale. To explain further let us work through an imaginary exercise.

Let us suppose you are making a white, dry table wine. You need eleven per cent alcohol, which means a starting gravity of 1083. The original must reads 1015 on the scale and so you will need to add sufficient sugar to reach 1083 (see

GRAVITY READINGS, SUGAR CONTENT AND POTENTIAL ALCOHOL

Specific Gravity	Amount of sugar in 1 gallon (ounces)
1.010	2
1.015	4
1.020	7
1.025	9
1.030	12
1.035	15
1.040	17
1.045	19
1.050	21
1.055	23
1.060	25
1.065	27
1.070	29
1.075	31
1.080	33
1.085	36
1.090	38
1.095	40
1.100	42
1.105	44
1.110	46
1.115	48
1.120	50
1.125	52
1.130	54
1.135	56

Table data reproduced from *First Steps in W*

The above table shows the correlation between hydrometer readings, sugar content and alcohol potential.

of sugar in (grammes)	Potential % Alcohol by vol.
55	0.9
125	1.6
195	2.3
265	3.0
320	3.7
410	4.4
480	5.1
535	5.8
590	6.5
645	7.2
705	7.8
760	8.6
815	9.2
870	9.9
930	10.6
1010	11.3
1065	12.0
1125	12.7
1180	13.4
1235	14.1
1290	14.9
1345	15.6
1400	16.3
1455	17.0
1510	17.7
1565	18.4

Berry, by kind permission of Argus Books

Close-up of a hydrometer reading.

the table provided). There is a difference of 68 points of gravity, and by referring to the table you can see that an additional one pound twelve ounces of sugar is needed.

When making dessert wines, it is, as has already been mentioned, advisable to add only some of the sugar at the start in order not to over-work the yeast, and to add the rest of the sugar in small doses. The hydrometer is vital when feeding a wine with sugar. If you add a small amount of sugar syrup daily you must keep a constant check on the gravity readings. Only in this way can you be sure that the yeast is still working and that you will not be left with a stuck fermentation. If the gravity fails to fall after a day, discontinue adding the syrup.

The hydrometer is equally useful in beermaking. It is used to check that the starting gravity of the wort is right to produce the correct alcoholic strength of that type of beer, to check on the progress of the fermentation by recording the gradual but steady drop in the specific gravity, and to help you judge when the beer is ready for bottling or kegging. If the beer is bottled at too high a gravity, burst bottles may result, or at best you will have a beer too highly charged with gas and your tankard will be full of nothing but foam. Ordinary milds, lagers, and light ales usually have original gravities of 1030-1040, stouts, bitters, and pale ales 1035-1050, and barley wine anything up to 1080. Bottling is commonly at gravities of 1000-1010, depending on the beer style. A heavy barley wine will not fall as low as 1000, but this would be normal for a light ale or light lager.

When checking a sample of fermenting of very young wine or beer, spin the hydrometer in the trial jar to dispel the bubbles of carbon dioxide that will cling to it, otherwise the gas bubbles will buoy up the hydrometer and give a false reading. The saccharometer is virtually identical to the hydrometer. Translated from its Latin roots its name means sugar measure. It is sometimes coded in bands of colour instead of numbers.

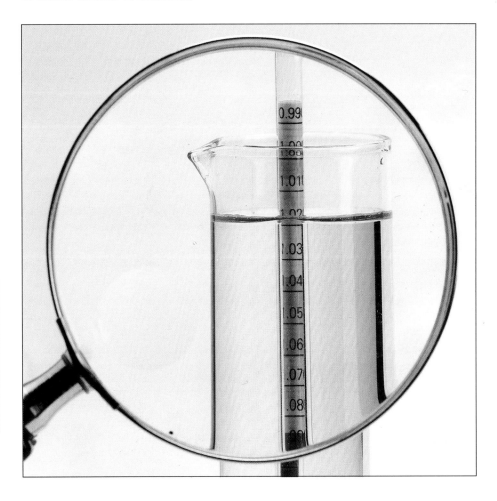

Grape Juice Concentrate and Kit Wines

1

The one section that has not yet been covered is probably the principal method most of us employ when we start making wines. This is by purchasing a kit, or a container of grape juice concentrate. These are in fact very different articles will be covered separately.

Firstly, grape juice concentrate. This is a very rich liquid produced by squeezing the juice from the grapes and then extracting much of the water, leaving only the solids and soluble materials. It is produced in wine-making countries and is available to make all colours and styles of wine, and has many uses for our hobby. It is possible to produce a gallon of wine purely from a can or bottle of concentrate, and all instructions are invariably supplied with the container. All that is necessary to add is the water, sugar in most cases, and additives. The end product is basic and drinkable, but one should never forget that this juice is not made from grade one wine grapes. More often than not it is the unwanted grapes, those of poorer quality, that the producers turn into concentrate.

2

The one thing that cannot be argued is that you get what you pay for. If you buy a cheap grape concentrate, and expect it to result in a good table wine, you will probably be disappointed. If, however, you purchase a well known, branded, good quality product, you will stand a better chance of success. A quality test on the Vigneron range of 'Director's Choice' wines gave a very impressive result, particularly for the 'Chateau Rich Red' wine.

There are also powdered grape concentrates on sale. I have never tried these, but I do wonder what is left after so much has been extracted.

The second, and in my opinion the better, use for concentrates is as an ingredient with other fruits or vegetables to act as a boost to the must. In this case the quality of the product is not quite so important, as you are only using it as a minor ingredient. It does help to give the wine a better bouquet, and will give the extra body needed when making good quality wine. It is possible to replace items in recipes, such as sultanas or raisins, with grape concentrate because, of course, these are simply dried grapes.

3

The other kind of kit is one which contains fruits or fruit juices. These also come in different categories, but the instructions are generally very explicit. Some of these claim that it is possible to produce six bottles of wine in three weeks. This is quite correct, and if the instructions are followed to the letter anyone can achieve this. It must be remembered, however, that in order to produce wine in just three weeks the manufacturers have to use a great range of chemicals. The side effects of these chemicals will unfortunately be noticeable in both the bouquet and taste. Again it is rather obvious that you get what you pay for, and although these quick wines have a place in our hobby, the results are generally disappointing.

The fruit concentrates you can buy to make a gallon of wine, using the normal time schedule, are in some cases very good and well worth buying. There are available some excellent 'hock' style packages made by well known manufacturers such as Unican, and there are good French style kit wines too. If the instructions are followed carefully the results should be satisfactory. If, however, you wish to experiment, you can either add to the initial must or deduct from it. Whatever you do, whatever you add or deduct, or if you use less water, do keep a record of all variations. It is almost certain that you will not remember the details should you wish to make a repeat batch of wine.

There are also packages available with which you can imitate such drinks as Sherry or Vermouth. These are generally of excellent quality and result in a very pleasant end product. They are not cheap but are, in my opinion, extremely good value for money. Again it is possible to adapt the kits to one's own requirements. It is often helpful to add a bottle of a commercial branded wine to a gallon of one of the home-brewed products to give it more of the characteristics of the type.

At most major competitive shows around the country there are classes specifically for wines made using the above styles of ingredients. If these are not included, you can of course enter kit or concentrate wines into any suitable classes, but it is unusual for one to succeed over a really well-made, fresh-ingredient wine.

To sum up, these wines definitely have a place. Often they are the first step towards becoming involved in winemaking, and can also fill a gap when we are running out of drinkable wine. They can be very useful when balancing a must of fresh ingredients. It is, however, recommended that you do not remain with these wines alone; that you try your hand at winemaking with other ingredients.

Stages in kit wine making: (1) cleaning and sterilizing the demijohn; (2) pouring the concentrate into the sterilized demijohn; (3) adding liquid to the airlock; (4) fermentation taking place, aided by an electric thermal belt; (5) racking into a clean jar; (6) corking the filled bottles; (7) putting seals on the necks; (8) steaming the seal onto the neck of the bottle.

Spring Wine

Flower Wines

When the long winter is over, and the countryside is awakening, there is the temptation to explore, and perhaps to gather wild ingredients. April 23rd is St George's Day, when by tradition dandelions are picked for the first gallon of the year.

There are, however, points to think about when collecting the flowers. Where are they growing? Near a main road? Then they may be contaminated with diesel fumes, rubber or road dust generally. In the heart of the country? They may have been sprayed with weed killer or insecticide. A little research is necessary, but country folk, generally winemakers themselves, will usually prove very helpful. As far as I am aware, all dandelions are suitable for winemaking, but it is only the yellow petals that are used. The green parts of the plant contain a latex that gives a bitter taste to the wine, and they should be left out. Wherever they are picked, the dandelion petals will still be dusty, and a short rinse in a weak mixture of sodium metabisulphite, or one Campden tablet to a pint of water, is recommended.

All flowers should be picked when the petals are dry, preferably when the sun is on them. The reasons for this are twofold. Dry florets weigh much less than wet ones, so a more accurate measure is obtained. With the sun on the bloom it will have opened to its maximum, the nectar and perfume flow will be at their height, and this means that the greatest bouquet and flavour can be obtained. The Mayblossom of the hawthorn tree is a perfect example of this, as the tiny florets open into miniature circles, giving off a heavenly scent. If a May tree is found with pink blossom, a really exquisite pale rosé wine can be made from the flowers; ingredients to make rosé wines are not easy to find. The best known of all the flowers for winemaking, the elderflower, probably has the greatest number of hazards for the winemaker. There are many different varieties of the one species of elder native to Great Britain, and there are a few imported ornamental species as well, but only a few are really suitable for winemaking. Some of the pitfalls will be explained in the elderflower wine recipe that follows, but take note also of the colour of the flowers. As they get older, so they darken and become a dull cream. This means they have lost their freshness and should be avoided. There are many views on how much or how many elderflowers are required; my recipe says three large heads of florets are sufficient, but other authors quote up to a quart (roughly one litre) of flowers. If you are making elderflower wine to drink as it is, then my recommendation is sufficient. If, however, you intend to use your wine to add to other wines to increase their bouquet or flavour, then naturally a more intense and concentrated wine is required. One important thing to remember when making flower wines is that usually only bouquet, and to a lesser extent flavour and colour, can be extracted from the blooms. Unless the aim is to make a very light, flowery wine, extra body must be added in the form of grape concentrate or dried fruit such as sultanas. It is not advisable to use anything which has a strong flavour or smell, as this will overpower the delicate flower content. Acid, nutrient salts, and tannin will also have to be added, as they are not supplied by the flowers, and without them an unbalanced wine will result.

Flowers gathered for winemaking should not be collected into a polythene bag, as this will cause them to sweat and rapidly spoil. Put them in a basket or tray, or at worst a coarse brown paper bag, and leave the top open for them to respire.

Dried flowers are a very useful standby for the winery cupboard, to be used either as a main ingredient, or as an addition to improve a wine must. They can be purchased from winemaking, health food, and some chemists' shops, and come in quite a wide variety, many that the winemaker could not gather. Dried flowers are highly concentrated, and 2 ounces/60 grams is usually sufficient to make a gallon of wine. If you have roses in your garden and you want to collect the petals, the time to pick them is when they are in full flush, just before they fall. It is possible to collect these gradually and freeze them, until enough have been collected. If you buy dried dandelions you will find that whole heads, including the once-green parts, are included. This is quite acceptable; drying the flowers takes away the bitter substance that would otherwise spoil your wine.

Dried Fruit

Wine can be produced throughout the year from the various dried fruits that are available. The most obvious range includes raisins and sultanas, which of course are dried grapes of different types. These do contain all the ingredients needed to make wine, if used in sufficient quantity, but it is usual to use these fruits in conjunction with other ingredients. They have been dried and concentrated from their original state and are therefore stronger than the fresh ingredients. Generally the rule is that a quarter of a pound of dried fruit is equal to a pound of fresh fruit. During the drying stage the skins of these fruits has toughened, and it is preferable to mince or chop them coarsely before adding them to our must. This not only helps the yeast to extract the natural sugars and acids present in the fruit, but prevents them swelling up in the liquid. Left unbroken, the dried grapes would absorb a lot of liquid and when thrown away they would take a lot of valuable fermentable sugar, and flavour and bouquet forming compounds with them. The one disadvantage that they have is that most are strongly flavoured, and cannot be used in delicate light wines, or wines where the flavour and bouquet of the main ingredient, such as red currant, is meant to come through.

It is always advisable to rinse the fruit in a bowl of hot water, to remove dust and any coating, such as paraffin oil. This is commonly used to give the fruit a glistening, attractive appearance and prevent the formation of unsightly sugar crystals on the surface.

Peaches, apricots, apples and plums (prunes) are examples of other dried fruits that can be used in winemaking. They should also be rinsed in hot water, to wash away any dust and sulphur compounds, or similar preservatives, which are used to prevent the fruit darkening and to extend its useful storage life.

Another range of dried fruit very useful to the winemaker is dried country fruit. As the actual picking time for elderberries is so limited, the use of the dried version is a bonus. Bilberries are also available in this form, rather expensive but very acceptable. Again, dried fruit is four times the strength of the equivalent fresh fruit. When making a heavy dessert wine the main requirements are full body and high alcohol. Some experts feel that as much as 18 or 20 lbs of fruit is the minimum if these aims are to be achieved. To collect and prepare sufficient fresh fruit to follow this example would be very time consuming and laborious, but it is possible to use dried ingredients together with fresh. It is in these instances that dried dates, figs, and bananas are so useful. These ingredients, again at a quarter the quantity of fresh fruit, can add substantial body and natural sugar to achieve the required standards, and not increase the natural fruit acid content of the wine to an excessive amount.

Birch Sap Wine. The recipe for birch sap wine is an interesting experiment, and if carried out correctly will do no harm to the trees. It is very important to plug the hole afterwards to prevent the sap from continuing to leak. The flavour of the wine is aperitif or dry sherry style, and although the recipe is for a dry wine, it can be sweetened up after completion. Apart from maple, sycamore and walnut, saps are not usually used in winemaking, except in Greece. There, the resin of a pine tree is added to the grape wine in the making of Retsina. And in the author's view, for her taste it can stay in Greece.

Dandelion

Medium Dry White Table Wine

4pts/2.5ltrs dandelion flower heads
2¼lbs/1kg white sugar
1tsp/5g citric acid
1tsp/5g yeast nutrient
1 packet medium white wine yeast
2 oranges
½lb/225g sultanas

Cut off the yellow parts of the flower heads, discarding the green portions, which would give the wine a bitter aftertaste and hinder the fermentation. **(1)** Pour 5 pints/2.5 litres of boiling water over the flower heads, chopped sultanas, and the orange segments – don't include the pith. Leave for 2 days, stirring at least twice daily. On the third day stir the yeast and a teaspoon of sugar into half a cup of warm water. Bring to the boil in 1 pint/0.5 litre of water, cool, and then pour the syrup into a demijohn. **(2)** Strain off the flowers, orange and sultana fragments, and add the liquid, and the acid and nutrient dissolved in a little warm water. Top up the demijohn to the shoulder with cold water. Add the yeast culture, and agitate vigorously. Fit a rubber bung and half-filled airlock, and leave in a warm place, shaking daily until fermentation is completed. Rack the wine into a clean jar, top up with apple juice or cool water, and add a crushed Campden tablet. Refit bung and airlock, and leave to mature in a cool place, racking at three-monthly intervals.

This wine is drinkable in 9 months, but is better left for a year.

❑ *Remember, St George's Day, 23rd April, is the traditional day to start picking dandelions.*

1

2

May Blossom

(Hawthorn flower)

Dry White Table Wine

1gal/4.5ltrs May blossom, white or pink

2½lb/1.1kg sugar

---

2 oranges

---

2 lemons

1tsp/5g grape tannin powder

Wine yeast and 1tsp/5g nutrient salts.

Water to 1gal/4.5ltrs

---

(1) For the best results, put the flowers in a muslin bag, which can be placed in a large pan in 7 pints/4 litres of water, and simmered for a quarter of an hour. Then squeeze the bag well, to extract all the liquid, and discard the bag and its contents. **(2)** Dissolve the sugar in the hot liquid, and add the juice and zest of the oranges and lemons. (The zest is the coloured part of the skin, without any white pith.) Allow the liquor to cool to 21°C (70°F), then add the tannin, general purpose wine yeast, and yeast nutrient. Cover well. Three days is sufficient for fermentation to get well under way if the must is kept in a warm place and given a daily stir. Then strain it into a fermenting jar, top up to the shoulder with cool water, fit a bung and airlock, and leave the jar in a slightly cooler place for the fermentation to be completed. Rack it (syphon it off the lees) after three months, when a sediment will have formed. Put it in a cooler place still; it will be ready to drink after another three months or so. Then rack it again, add a crushed Campden tablet, and top up the level to the neck of the jar with water.

❑ *If the 'pink' May blossom is used, the end product will be a delicate rosé wine.*

1

2

Elderflower
Medium Dry White Table Wine

3 large heads of elderflower florets

¼ pt/140ml white grape concentrate

2¼ lbs/1kg white sugar

1tsp/5g citric acid

1tsp/5g yeast nutrient

1tsp/5g grape tannin or cup of strong tea

Wine yeast

Check before you pick the flowers that they are a variety suitable for winemaking, as some have a very unpleasant smell. They should be light and fragrantly scented, not 'catty'. Pinch a floret between your fingers and check the nose; this is the bouquet the finished wine will have. Always pick when the sun is out, and the flowers are dry and fully open. Strip the florets from the stalks and place them in a bucket. Add 5 pints/2.5 litres of boiling water and leave covered for two days, stirring at least twice daily. From the third day, proceed as for the Dandelion Wine recipe.

Never be tempted to use a greater quantity of elderflower than your recipe calls for. Elderflowers are easily gathered, but too much in a wine will spoil it, as it has such a strong bouquet.

❏ *Elderflowers can also be used as an extra ingredient when making other wines. Just a pinch or two of the florets can enhance any bouquet. The florets can be placed in plastic bags and frozen while fresh for this purpose.*

Orange Blossom and Grape Concentrate

Medium Sweet White Table Wine

2oz/60g dried orange blossom
1 750ml bottle Roses lime juice
2lb/1kg can white grape concentrate
1tsp/5g pectic enzyme
1tsp/5g yeast nutrient
Burgundy wine yeast
1lb/450 g white sugar

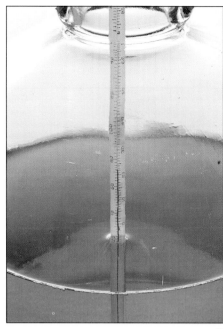

1   **2**

Activate the yeast by preparing a yeast starter before making up the must.

Dissolve the sugar in 1 pint/0.5 litre of boiling water. **(1)** When cool, pour the sugar syrup, grape concentrate, and lime juice into a demijohn. **(2)** Add 3 pints/ 1.5 litres of water, and agitate well to mix contents. **(3)** Add the pectic enzyme, nutrient, yeast starter, **(4)** and orange blossom, **(5)** and fit bung and airlock. Leave in a warm place, shaking the jar daily. After seven days, strain out the orange blossom and top up the jar with cool water to the shoulder. Refit the airlock and leave to ferment until the wine is clear. Add a crushed Campden tablet, then on the next day rack off any sediment of yeast cells into a clean jar, and refit the airlock. Leave the wine to mature in the cool, racking again after three months if further sediment occurs.

Serve this wine slightly chilled.

❑ ***There is a considerable range of dried flower petals available from winemaking shops. This recipe can be adapted to use them.***

3

4

5

Sweet Basil and Rosehip

Medium Light Table Wine

2pts/1ltr fresh Sweet Basil leaves, or
2oz/60g dried leaves
6oz/175g dried rosehips or rosehip shells
2 oranges and 2 lemons
1tsp/5g tannin
1tsp/5g pectic enzyme
1tsp/5g tronozymol yeast nutrient
2¼lb/1kg white sugar
General purpose wine yeast

(1) Rinse the leaves and chop them coarsely. Place in a saucepan or boiler with the rosehips and 4 pints/2 litres of boiling water, then remove the pan from the heat. **(2)** Leave overnight to infuse, as in making tea. Dissolve the sugar in 1 pint/0.5 litre of boiling water, and add the syrup to the fermentation vessel. **(3)** Add the strained Sweet Basil and rosehip liquor and the orange and lemon juice, cover, and leave to cool. When down to about 21°C (70°F), add the pectic enzyme, activated yeast, yeast nutrient, and zest.

Cover the fermentation vessel, keeping it in a warm place. Stir daily, and after seven days fermentation, **(4)** strain the must into a 1 gallon/4.5 litre fermentation jar. Top up with cool water to the neck of the jar, and fit a bored bung and airlock. Leave to ferment and when the wine falls clear, syphon it from the yeast and other debris into another clean jar. Add a crushed Campden tablet and mature for a few months.

A 2 pint/1 litre carton of pure apple, grapefruit, or orange juice can be added to the starting must, to give the wine more body and vary the flavour. The water content must be adjusted to compensate, partly by dissolving the sugar in some of the Sweet Basil liquor.

❏ *You can substitute fresh or frozen rosehips, but remember you will need four times as many.*

1

2

3

4

1

Parsley

Dry White Table Wine

1lb/0.5kg fresh parsley or 2oz/60g
dried parsley.
2½lb/1.1kg white sugar
½pt/280ml white grape concentrate
2 oranges
1tsp/5g citric acid
1tsp/5g grape tannin
1tsp/5g yeast nutrient
1tsp/5g all-purpose yeast

2

3

Start the yeast in a starter bottle during the previous day. Dissolve the sugar in 1 pint/0.5 litre of boiling water, and leave under a cover to cool. **(1)** Soak the chopped parsley for twenty-four hours with the juice and zest of the oranges in 4 pints/2.25 litres of water. Then bring to the boil and simmer for twenty minutes, cool and **(2)** strain into a demijohn. **(3)** Add the sugar syrup, grape concentrate, and other ingredients, top up to the shoulder of the jar with cool water. Pour in the yeast starter, and fit the bung and airlock. Leave to ferment in a warm place, shaking daily for the first week.

When fermentation has ceased, leave to settle in a cool place before racking. Add one crushed Campden tablet at the first racking.

This wine is very nice if left to ferment to complete dryness and then served chilled. It can, however, be sweetened with grape concentrate and a teaspoon of potassium sorbate, or with a non-fermenting sweetener. This wine is a perfect stand-by that can be made at any time of the year.

❏ *I have known wine from this recipe win a dry white wine class at a large show. Give it a try, it is well worth it.*

1

Dried Elderberry

Dry Table Wine

2½lb/1.1kg dried elderberries
2lb/900g raisins, coarsely chopped
1½lb/675g sugar (dissolved in
1pt/0.5ltr boiling water)
1tsp/5g nutrient
1tsp/5g citric acid
1tsp/5g pectic enzyme
Beaujolais wine yeast (start it the previous day)
Water to 1gal./4.5ltr

(1) Soak the elderberries in 3 pints/
1.5 litres boiling water overnight. Crush
the berries **(2)** and strain off the liquid

into a bucket. Pour another 2 pints/1 litre
of boiling water on to the pulp, stir for
five minutes, and strain off the juice into
the bucket. Add the chopped raisins,
sugar syrup, nutrient and acid to the fruit
juice and stir. When cooled to 21°C
(70°F) add the yeast pectic enzyme and fit
the bung and airlock. After five days,
strain the must into a clean fermentation
jar. Top up to the shoulder of the jar with
tap water, or grape juice for a better
wine, and leave in a warm place to finish
fermenting. When the wine starts to clear,
and to throw a sediment, move the jar
into a cooler place.

Rack after a further two weeks, and
add a crushed Campden tablet. Replace
the airlock, and leave the wine to mature
for at least a year, racking occasionally if
a sediment forms.

❏ ***Do not leave the ingredients in
the must any longer than stated,
or the wine will be unbalanced by
excess tannin.***

2

Fig and Rosehip

Medium Sweet Social Wine

1lb/450g dried figs
½lb/225g dried rosehips or rosehip shells
1½lb/675g sugar
1tsp/5g citric acid
1tsp/5g pectic enzyme
1tsp/5g nutrient
Tokay wine yeast

(1) Chop the figs into coarse pieces, **(2)** place into a white plastic fermentation bucket with the dried rosehips, cover with 5 pints/2.5 litres of boiling water and leave to soak overnight. **(3)** Next day boil the sugar in 1 pint/0.5 litre of water and add it to the bucket. Add the acid, pectic enzyme and nutrient, stir well, cover, and leave for twelve hours. Meanwhile, start the yeast in a bottle with ½pint/280 ml warm water and 2 teaspoons/10 grams of sugar, plugged with cotton wool. Add the yeast to the bucket at the end of the twelve hours. Leave the bucket in a warm place, covered, for seven days, stirring daily. Then strain into a demijohn, fit an airlock, and leave for the fermentation to finish. Transfer to a cool place when the wine starts clearing, and rack off when a sediment forms. Add a crushed Campden tablet and leave for several months to mature. Sweeten to taste and add a teaspoon of potassium sorbate as a stabiliser.

This wine may need to be racked several times, as it clears quite slowly. Top up each time with apple juice or grape juice.

❏ *If you find difficulty in obtaining dried rosehips or rosehip shells, replace them with rosehip syrup.*

1

2

3

Apricot and Grape concentrate

Dry White Table Wine

½lb/225g dried apricots
½pint/280ml white grape concentrate
½tsp/3g citric acid
½tsp/3g tannin
1tsp/5g pectic enzyme
1tsp/5g yeast nutrient
1tsp/5g general purpose yeast
2lb/900g sugar

Make a starter bottle with the yeast, half a pint of lukewarm water and two teaspoons of sugar. **(1)** Place the apricots in a bucket or large bowl, and scald them with a kettle of boiling water. Leave to soak for a couple of minutes, then drain them through a colander, discarding the liquid. Coarsely chop the fruit, put it in the bucket with the sugar. **(2)** Add 3 pints/1.5 litres of hot water, and stir well to dissolve the sugar.

When cool, add the activated yeast and the rest of the ingredients, and 2 pints/1 litre of cold water. Cover and leave for seven days, stirring daily. Then strain gently through a nylon sieve; rinse the pulp with a little lukewarm water, and use the liquid to top up the jar to the gallon. **(3)** Fit the airlock, and leave the jar in a warm place to ferment out in the ordinary way. Rack as necessary.

Ready to drink in 9 months to 1 year.

This recipe can be converted into a social wine by using 1 pound/450 grams of apricots.

❑ *If the finished wine is too dry, sweeten it with a wine sweetener, not with sugar.*

1

2

3

Date and Banana

Medium Sweet Social Wine

2lb/900g chopped dates
1lb/450g ripe bananas
2lb/900g sugar, boiled until clear in
1 pint of water.
1 cup cold tea
1tsp/5g citric acid
1tsp/5g yeast nutrient
1tsp/5g pectic enzyme
1tsp/5g general purpose yeast

(1) Peel and slice the bananas and place them in a saucepan with 2 pints/1 litre of water. Bring to the boil, simmer for twenty minutes, then strain them into a jug, retaining the fluid. Mince or chop the dates and place them in a white plastic bucket. Add the sugar syrup, the banana 'gravy' and the tea, and 2 pints/1 litre of cold water. When cool (21°C or 70°F), add the acid, nutrient, and pectic enzyme, and stir well. Put the yeast in a bottle, add ½pint/280 ml of tepid water, shake well, and add to the bucket twelve hours later.

Keep in a warm place, stirring daily for seven days, then strain into a demijohn. Top up with water as necessary, fit an airlock, and return to the warm until the fermentation has ceased. Rack into a clean jar when a sediment has formed, sweeten to taste and top up, refit the airlock, and place in a clear place to settle. When the wine clears, rack again, add a crushed Campden tablet. Rack again if and when necessary.

❏ *Ripe bananas can be kept in a freezer until required. A visit to a market at closing time can often be beneficial in obtaining them at a very low cost.*

1

Dried Fruit

Medium Dry White Table Wine

2lb/900g sultanas
1lb/450g large raisins
2½lb/1.1 kg sugar
1 orange
1 lemon
1tsp/5g pectic enzyme
1tsp/5g yeast nutrient
Tokay wine yeast

(1) Chop the fruit and put it in a plastic bucket with the zest and juice of the orange and lemon, being careful not to include any pith. **(2)** Add the sugar, and pour on 6 pints/3 litres of boiling water, stirring thoroughly with a wooden or plastic spoon to dissolve the sugar. Cover, and leave to cool to about 21°C (70°F). Add the pectic enzyme and a crushed

Campden tablet, cover again, and leave for twenty-four hours. Then add the nutrient and yeast starter, and re-cover. Keep in a warm room, stirring daily for ten days.

(3) Next strain the liquid into a fermentation jar, top up to the shoulder with water, and fit the airlock. Leave the jar in the warm until the wine ferments to dryness. **(4)** Rack off the sediment, add a crushed Campden tablet, top up to a gallon with cold water, and leave to clear before bottling.

Further racking may be needed with this wine, and it should not stand for more than a few days on any build-up of sediment. **(5)** Top up with white grape juice or apple juice.

The wine should be ready to drink in six months, but it will improve if you leave it longer.

❏ *To make this wine as an aperitif the dried fruit can be substituted by packets of mixed fruit containing chopped peel. Remember to wash the fruit thoroughly before use.*

2

3

Tea

Dry Table Wine

4tbsps loose tea leaves or 8-12 teabags
1lb/450g chopped raisins or sultanas
1 medium orange
1 medium lemon
1tsp/5g yeast nutrient
Activated general purpose or sherry yeast
2½lb/1.1kg sugar

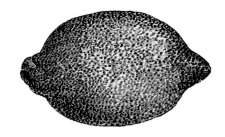

Make up 6 pints3 litres of tea, and strain this while still hot into a fermenting bucket. **(1)** Stir in and dissolve the sugar with a plastic or wooden spoon. Wash and chop the raisins or sultanas (or a mixture of the two) and add to the bucket with the juice and zest (no pith) of the orange and lemon. When cool, add the nutrient, yeast starter, and pectic enzyme. Cover and set aside in the warm to ferment for seven days, stirring daily.

Strain the must into a clean glass demijohn, top up with cool tea, fit the airlock, and leave to ferment to dry. Then rack from the lees, add a crushed Campden tablet, and leave to clear before bottling.

A dry tea wine is useful for blending with other wines that may seem a little flat or dull due to a low tannin content.

Different teas will give milder or more robust flavours to this type of wine; experiment with Earl Grey and other delicate teas. The finished wine is characteristic of the initial tea used.

❑ *A wine to make at any time of the year, perhaps when other ingredients are not readily available.*

4

5

1

Orange and Apple

Everyday Basic Table Wine

4pts/2ltrs natural orange juice
2pts/1ltr natural apple juice
1½lb/675g sugar, boiled with 1pt/0.5ltr water
1tsp/5g citric acid
1tsp/5g grape tannin
1tsp/5g yeast nutrient
1tsp/5g all-purpose yeast made into a starter bottle

Fruit juices are sold in most large grocers and supermarkets, in cartons; avoid any that contain preservatives. **(1)** Pour the two juices into a demijohn with the **(2)** sugar syrup and other additives. Fit an airlock, and after twelve hours add the pre-started yeast. **(3)** Top up with water to the shoulder of the jar, refit the airlock, and leave the wine in the warm to ferment to dryness. Shake daily to encourage fermentation. If you are using an electric heating tray, take care that the base of the jar does not get too hot.

Place the wine in the cool, where it will settle and clear very quickly. Rack as soon as a sediment has formed, and add a crushed Campden tablet. Rack twice more as and when needed, but do not add any more Campden tablets. **(4)** Top up each time with apple juice.

This wine is drinkable in three months, and does not improve greatly with keeping. It is a very good recipe for making 'plonk' to drink while other and better wines mature. It is also a very good recipe for the novice to try and the author often uses it to demonstrate winemaking to beginners at local clubs.

Be adventurous and try different fruit juices using this as a base recipe. Grape-fruit wine is very pleasant, especially for summer drinking, as is passion fruit wine, which is better slightly sweetened. If making wine from grape juice, use three litres, and omit the apple juice.

❑ **Do not confuse fresh grape juice with the canned, concentrated grape juice sold by homebrew shops.**

1

2

3

4

Seville Orange

Sweet Aperitif

1lb 14oz/850g tin of 'Mamade' brand prepared marmalade oranges
½lb/225g sultanas
2oz/60g dates
2lb/900g sugar (initially)
¼tsp/1g malic acid
½tsp/3g tartaric acid
1tsp/5g yeast nutrient
2tsp/10g pectic enzyme
Tokay yeast; activated at least 12 hours before

1

Wash and mince sultanas and dates. **(1)** Place in a bucket with the marmalade oranges and **(2)** pour on 5 pints/ 2.5 litres of cooled boiled water. Add pectic enzyme and 2 crushed Campden tablets, cover and leave for twenty-four hours in a warm place. Dissolve the sugar in a pint of boiling water. Allow to cool, then add to the bucket with the remainder of the ingredients and yeast, and ferment for four days, stirring twice daily.
(3) Strain into a demijohn and fit an airlock. Rack off any sediment after ten days, and check the specific gravity. As soon as it is down to SG 1010, add 4 ounces /112 grammes of sugar dissolved in a little hot water. Repeat this process as many times as possible, slowly raising the alcohol content to the maximum. Rack after one month, and again at three months. When the fermentation has ended, rack again, sweeten to taste, and add a crushed Campden tablet and a teaspoonful of potassium sorbate to prevent re-fermentation. Store in bulk for a year before bottling.

It is recommended that this wine is sweetened, as suggested.

Because it is made from Seville oranges, it may be rather bitter to drink as a dry wine.

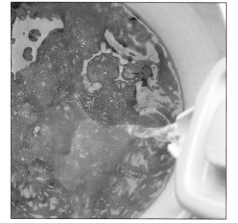

2

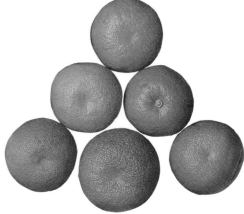

3

❏ *Fresh oranges are not suitable as an alternative.*

Gooseberry and Apricot

Dry White Table Wine

1½ lb/680g tin of gooseberries in syrup
½ lb/225g tinned or fresh apricots, or
4oz/112g dried
1lb/450g bananas
½ pint/280ml white grape concentrate
½ tsp/3g citric acid
½ tsp/3g grape tannin
1tsp/5g yeast nutrient
Activated general purpose yeast
1tsp/5g pectic enzyme
2¼ lb/1kg sugar

1

2

3

4

5

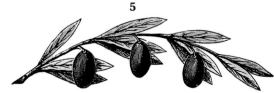

6

(1) Place the gooseberries and syrup in the fermentation bucket, macerating them as you do so. Stone the apricots if fresh, and crush them, together with the gooseberries. Peel the bananas, cut them into small pieces, and simmer with 2 pints/1 litre of water in a saucepan for twenty minutes, **(2)** then tip the pan's contents into the bucket. Stir in the sugar with a wooden spoon until dissolved. **(3)** When cool, (21°C, 70°F) add the rest of the ingredients and yeast and 3 pints/ 1.5 litres of cold water. **(4)** Cover closely, and keep in a warm spot, stirring daily.

(5) After seven days, strain through a nylon sieve over a funnel into a 1 gallon/ 4.5 litre glass jar, or demijohn, **(6)** topping up to the shoulder of the jar by 'washing' the pulp with lukewarm water. Fit an airlock and leave to ferment to completion in the usual way. Rack from the lees when the fermentation has ended, add a crushed Campden tablet, and leave the wine to clear before bottling.

❏ *Other tinned fruits can be used, but remember the finished wine will have the characteristics of the ingredients.*

1

2

3

4

5

6

Ribena or Blackcurrant

Sweet Social Wine

1 x 24fl. oz/600ml bottle of Ribena
Blackcurrant syrup
6lb/2.75kg sugar
1tsp/5g citric acid
2tsp/10g yeast nutrient
2tsp/10g all-purpose yeast

To make 2 gallons/9 litres of wine, **(1)** put the sugar and blackcurrant juice in a large saucepan with 6 pints/3 litres of water and **(2)** bring to the boil. Simmer for ten minutes to drive off any preservative in the juice. **(3)** Allow to cool, then pour through a funnel into two demijohns, **(4)** and top up to the shoulder with cold water. **(5)** Put in the yeast and other additives **(6)** and fit bungs and airlocks. Leave in a warm place for fermentation to take place. After two weeks or so, when the initial fermentation has died down a little, top up with cold water to the bottom of the neck of the jars and replace the airlocks. Then continue the fermentation in the usual way. When the fermentation has ended, rack the wine and add a crushed Campden tablet to each jar, bottling the wine when it is clear and stable. Sweeten if necessary with a non-fermenting sweetener such as Vinsweet or Canderel. If preferred, half a bottle of Ribena can be used to make just one gallon of wine. Halve all the other quantities mentioned above, and proceed in the same way.

❑ *There is a slight risk with this recipe that the colour may fade. As a precaution I suggest using a dark glass demijohn, or covering a white one with brown paper when storing the wine.*

Bilberry

Dry Red Table Wine, Burgundy Style

2lb/900g bottled bilberries
½lb/225g minced or chopped sultanas
1 large juicy lemon
1 large juicy orange
2lb/900g sugar
¼tsp/1g malic acid
1tsp/5g pectic enzyme
1tsp/5g yeast nutrient
Burgundy wine yeast

Prepare the yeast starter in advance. Place the bilberries and their syrup, together with the sultanas, lemon and orange juice and zest (no bitter white pith) into the initial fermentation vessel. Add five pints of hot water and the sugar; stir well to dissolve the sugar When cool (21°C, 70°F), add the malic acid, pectic enzyme, nutrient, and activated yeast.

1

2

Cover and set aside to ferment for five days, stirring daily, **(1)** then strain through a nylon sieve placed over a large funnel stood in the neck of a demijohn. **(2)** Top up as necessary to the shoulder of the jar, sprinkling lukewarm water over the berries and sultana pulp in the sieve. **(3)** Fit a bung and airlock, and leave the must to ferment to completion.

When the ferment ends and the wine falls clear, rack it off the sediment, add a crushed Campden tablet, and top up the jar to the neck with cool water. Leave at least a month or so to mature, longer if possible.

This wine recipe has been made up repeatedly for well over a decade to produce some first-class light red wines.

❑ *It is a pity to drink this wine too young; with a little maturity it complements a meal very well.*

3

Grapefruit

Medium Dry White Table Wine

1lb 3oz/540g tin of grapefruit segments in syrup

20fl. oz/0.5ltr (1 pint) pure grape juice

2lb/900g sugar

1tsp/5g pectic enzyme

1tsp/5g yeast nutrient

½tsp/3g grape tannin

Activated Bordeaux wine yeast

(1) Place the grapefruit and syrup in a fermentation bucket and crush the segments – it is easiest by hand – until the majority of the segments are broken. Add 3 pints/1.5 litres of boiling water. Dissolve the sugar by boiling it in a pint of water, and pour the solution into the bucket. Cover, and allow to cool to 21°C (70°F) before adding the grape juice (note – this is not grape concentrate), all the other ingredients and the yeast starter. Stir well, cover, and place in a warm room. Stir the contents daily for five days – no longer – then strain out the solids and put the liquid into a demijohn. Top up to the shoulder with cold water, and fit a bung and airlock. Rack when there is ¼ inch/6 mm of sediment at the bottom of the container, and top up with water as necessary. When the wine is clear, rack again, and add a crushed Campden tablet. Drink this wine while it is still young.

A wine that is very true to the taste of the ingredient. A lovely drink, served chilled on a summer's day.

❑ *This wine can be used as the basis for grapefruit champagne.*

1

Birch Sap Wine

Dry White Table Wine or Aperitif

5pts/2.5ltrs fresh birch sap.

1pt/0.5ltr white grape concentrate

1½lb/675g sugar

1tsp/5g citric acid

Sherry yeast, pre-activated

An unusual ingredient, but one which makes a good, well-balanced dry wine with a distinctive taste. It is easy to tap a tree when the sap is rising, normally during the latter half of March. Do not take more than a gallon of sap from any one tree, and be sure to plug the hole firmly afterwards, or the continuing loss of sap could kill the tree. Birch sap quickly deteriorates, so if necessary start the must with a pint or so of sap and add to it daily as the sap flow continues.

Boil the sugar in 1 pint/0.5 litre of water, and allow to cool. Boil the sap to sterilise it, and cool. Place all the ingredients except the yeast in a demijohn and fit a bung and airlock. After twelve hours add the activated yeast, and refit the airlock. Keep in a warm place during fermentation, shaking the jar occasionally. As the end of fermentation approaches, move the wine to a cooler place and leave it to clear. Rack as necessary, and add a crushed Campden tablet. This wine needs to be kept for at least a year to mature.

❏ *The rather distinctive flavour can be very suitable for an apertif style wine.*

Summer

This is the season of the soft fruits, and with the arrival of the 'pick your own' fruit farms, there is an abundance of ingredients available at low cost. These fruits, such as strawberries and raspberries, are very distinctive in their flavours, and of course these flavours will come through into the taste of the wine. For this reason they are most suited for use when making a social style wine, where the rich, strong taste is balanced by the alcohol and body. You can make strawberry, raspberry, or red and white currant wine by using 4 pounds (1.8 kilos) of any one of the fruits, when fully ripe, but as an alternative, and for a more balanced wine, try using fruit from a mixture of them all. The fact that the wine has a strong flavour makes it unsuitable for a table wine, but a mixture of these fruits can be used as part of the ingredients for a dessert wine.

The gooseberry is a quite different type of fruit. This is probably the nearest in content and character that we have to the grape. It can be used to produce two completely different styles of wine. When gooseberries are picked young and still green, the wine they make is very clean and fresh, with quite a high acid content. One of the best-known grapes of commerce is called the Sauvignon Blanc, and this is said to have a gooseberry taste and character. The author once tried to describe a gooseberry, through an interpreter, to a group of Bulgarian winemakers, who were not familiar with this fruit. She got as far as it being 'white, round, and hairy, with a top and tail', and then gave up!

The other type of wine made from this fruit uses ripe, plump, sweet gooseberries. These will make a delicious sweet 'Sauternes' style wine, and may even produce a very pale 'blush' tint if the red variety has been used. It is difficult to say how much sugar one would use to 4 pounds of fruit because it depends on the sweetness of the berries. It would be advisable to start with 1 pound (675 grams), and then add doses of sugar syrup until the required alcohol and sweetness is reached. This can be tested by use of the hydrometer.

The blackcurrant is also ripe at this time, and this is one of the most concentrated in flavour and acid of all our fruits. For this reason only 3 pounds (1.36 kilos) is used per gallon, instead of the usual 4 pounds. It also requires longer to mature – at least one year. Red or white currants can be substituted for some of the fruit if it is more convenient; the blackcurrant flavour will still dominate the wine. In the commercial world, the red Cabernet Sauvignon, famous in Bordeaux as one of the major grapes used in claret, is known to have a blackcurrant nose and flavour.

Hopefully the summer weather is warm and there is no risk of the fermentation cooling down and stopping. On the contrary, you should be careful not to place the fermenting vessel, the bucket or jar, in direct sunlight, as this could overheat or 'cook' the must. While the yeast is very active, the temperature inside the vessel is increased by the heat generated by the yeast activity, and does not need any help. Particularly during these months it is very important to stir or shake the vessel at least once daily to keep the temperature even throughout the must.

Chablis-Type Gooseberry

Dry White Table Wine

5lb/2.25kg really green gooseberries
1tsp/5g mixed citric/tartaric acid
1tsp/5g pectic enzyme
1tsp/5g yeast nutrient
Activated Chablis wine yeast
1½lb/675g white granulated sugar.

Prepare the yeast starter in advance of making the must. Wash and top the fruit, there is no need to tail it. **(1)** Place the gooseberries in the initial fermentation vessel, then roughly crush them or squeeze them open. If they have been frozen for 24 hours and then thawed, this is much easier. **(2)** Add the sugar, and pour in half a gallon (2.25 litres) of hot water. Stir well to dissolve the sugar. **(3)** When cool, 21°C (70°F) add the pectic enzyme, yeast nutrient and activated yeast. Cover, and set aside to ferment on the pulp for five days, stirring daily, then strain into a glass demijohn. Top up with more must as necessary, by washing the pulp through with cool, boiled water. Fit a bung and airlock and set aside to ferment out to completion. Rack from the lees in due course, when the wine falls star-bright clear. Leave to mature for at least twelve months.

This wine can be your 'pièce de résistance', and should turn out as a very dry table wine, true to colour with a faint tinge of green. But to achieve the colour the fruit must be absolutely green.

1

2

3

❑ *This is one of the author's favourite wines, but do not be tempted to reduce the maturation time.*

Strawberry

Pale Rosé Medium Table Wine

4lb/1.8kg ripe strawberries
2¼lb/1kg granulated sugar
1 lemon
1tsp/5g pectic enzyme
1tsp/5g yeast nutrient
All-purpose wine yeast
½ tsp/3g tannin or cup of strong tea

Use fully-ripe strawberries, even if they are a bit squashy. Remove the hulls and wash the strawberries to get rid of any earth or dust. Place the fruit in a clean white plastic bucket with the juice and zest of the lemon, the tannin or tea, and the sugar. Pour 6 pints/3.4 litres of boiling water over them. Mash the strawberries with a plastic spoon, and stir well to dissolve the sugar. Then cover the bucket and leave the contents to cool right down before adding a crushed

Campden tablet and the pectic enzyme. Re-cover, and leave in the warm for twenty-four hours. Then stir in the yeast and yeast nutrient. Cover again, and keep in warm surroundings, stirring daily, for one week.

The must is now ready to be strained into the fermentation jar, and have an airlock fitted. **(1)** Strain the juice off carefully, taking care not to squeeze any of the pulp through the straining cloth. Top up to the shoulder of the jar with cool boiled water. **(2)** Leave to ferment until nearly dry. Small amounts of sugar syrup stirred in now will revive the fermentation and increase the alcohol in the wine, but be careful not to over-sweeten. **(3)** When the fermentation has ended, rack, allow to clear, and bottle in the usual way.

This wine will fade if it is not stored in a cool, dark place. If this is impossible, wrap a piece of brown paper around each bottle to keep out the light. Keep the wine at least six months before drinking.

❑ **With 'pick-your-own' farms readily available, this is a 'must'.**

1

2

3

Mixed Summer Fruit Wine

Light Table Wine

The previous recipe can be made using any mixture of soft fruits, providing the total weight is 4 pounds/1.8 kilos. Following the method for strawberry wine, the illustrations show the processes which apply for any combination of soft fruits. You could use, for example, 2 pounds/900 grams of strawberries plus 1 pound/450 grams each of raspberries and red or white currants. If you use more than 1 pound/450 grams of currants, omit the lemon juice. Any of the raspberry-type fruits can be used. Record the quantities used for future reference.

❏ ***This is a perfect recipe for the owner of a small fruit garden.***

2

3

4

5

1

6

1

Vine-Pruning 'Folly'

Dry White Table Wine

**Prunings of young growth to fill one
2gal/9ltr bucket, lightly pressed**

2lb/900g sugar

Juice and zest of two lemons

1tsp/5g yeast nutrient

---

(1) Put the cuttings and leaves into the bucket, and pour onto them 5 pints/2.8 litres of boiling water. Let this stand for 48 hours, but turn it occasionally to submerge the top leaves and keep the prunings well under the surface. Keep closely covered. Pour off the liquid through a strainer into a demijohn, and press out or squeeze the leaves and tendrils. Then 'wash' the prunings with 1 pint/0.5 litre of hot water, and press again. Dissolve the sugar in a pint of boiling water, and add it to the demijohn when cooled. **(2)** Add the lemon, yeast, and nutrient, and fit a bung and airlock. Top up to the shoulder of the jar if necessary.

Leave to ferment right out in a warm place, in the usual way, and rack when necessary.

❑ *This is an ideal wine to make if you are growing vines, as it is made with the first early-summer prunings. The goodness is obtained from the sap in the young stems, leaves, and tendrils. Just think of all the wasted prunings in the vineyards of Europe.*

2

Blackcurrant

Strong Red Table Wine

3lb/1.36kg Blackcurrants

2½lb/1.1kg sugar

1 packet all-purpose yeast

1tsp/5g nutrient

1tsp/5g pectic enzyme

(1) Put the blackcurrants into a large bucket and crush them. Turn the sugar into syrup by bringing it to the boil in 1 pint/0.5 litre of water and pour, still boiling, onto the currants. Add 5 pints/ 2.8 litres of cold water, and leave to cool to about 21°C (70°F). Then add the pectic enzyme, and a day later the yeast and yeast nutrient. Keep closely covered for five days in a warm place, stirring daily. **(2)** Then strain the must into a demijohn. **(3)** Fit a bung and airlock, topping up with cool, boiled water if necessary. Let it stand until the fermentation ceases and the wine clears, usually in about three months. Rack off the sediment, and again if necessary as the wine matures. Keep for one year.

This recipe does not include added acid, as blackcurrants are high in natural citric acid and a little malic. If you have insufficient blackcurrants, you can use 2 pounds/900 grams of blackcurrants and 1 pound/450 grams of mixed red and white currants.

❑ *A useful wine to use as a blend with one that is lacking in acid.*

1

2

3

Pea Pod

White Table Wine

4lb/1.8kg empty pea pods
1lb/450g ripe bananas
2lb/900g sugar
½tsp/3g citric acid
½tsp/3g grape tannin, or cup of strong tea
1tsp/5g pectic enzyme
1tsp/5g yeast nutrient

(1) Wash the pea pods and chop them into small pieces. **(2)** Place the fragments in a pan with the peeled, sliced bananas and 4 pints/2.25 litres of water. Bring to the boil and simmer for 20 minutes, then strain and leave to settle with a cover on. Boil the sugar in a pint of water until it clears, then leave it to cool. **(3)** After 24 hours strain the pea and banana liquor through a fine cloth . **(4)** Pour it into a demijohn. Add the other ingredients, including the sugar syrup, then top up to the shoulder of the jar with lukewarm water. Add the yeast, fit a bung and airlock. Leave to ferment as usual. Be careful not to let a heavy sediment build up, but rack the wine frequently.

❑ **This is a recipe for the 'country wine' enthusiast, but not likely to win any major prizes.**

1

2

3

Orange and Banana

Dry White Table Wine

8 sweet oranges
2lb/1kg very ripe bananas
½ pint/280ml white grape concentrate
1½lb/675g sugar
1tsp/5g pectic enzyme
1tsp/5g yeast nutrient
½tsp/3g grape tannin
Bordeaux yeast

Activate the yeast ready for use.
(1) Squeeze the juice from the oranges.
(2) Peel and chop the bananas into chunks, and simmer them for thirty minutes in 2 pints/1 litre of water. Put the sugar in a bucket, and strain the boiling liquid onto it; stir well to dissolve the sugar. Add the orange juice and grape concentrate, nutrient and tannin, and stir again. Make up to 1 gallon/4.5 litres with cool, boiled water, add the yeast, and transfer to a demijohn. Fit a bung and air lock, and ferment out to dry, racking when the wine falls clear. Add a crushed Campden tablet, and mature for six months before bottling.

❑ *The comment 'very ripe' means just that; the blacker the bananas are, the sweeter they will be.*

1

4

2

Basic Mead

3lb/1.36kg honey for a dry mead, or
4lb/1.8kg honey for a medium sweet mead, or
5lb/2.25kg honey for a sweet mead
½tsp/3g tannin, or a cup of cold tea
2tsp/10g citric acid
1½tsp/8g yeast nutrient, or two nutrient tablets
Sherry type yeast

Prepare the yeast starter in advance, to activate the yeast. Place the honey in the initial fermentation vessel or bucket, and make up to 1 gallon/4.5 litres with hot water. Stir well with a long-handled wooden or plastic spoon until the honey is dissolved. When cool, 21°C (70°F), add the tannin, nutrient and acid, and stir well to dissolve, then add the activated yeast. Cover closely. **(1)** After seven days transfer to a demijohn, topping up to the shoulder with cooled, boiled water if necessary. Fit a bung and airlock and set aside in a warm place to ferment to completion. Rack from the lees in due course, when the mead falls star-bright.

This is a basic recipe, but one can experiment with honeys from different flowers. About 1 pound/450 grams of fruit is generally sufficient, but again it is a matter of your own choice. The fruit should be pulped in the bucket before the honey and hot water are added, and strained out when the must is transferred to the demijohn. If acidic fresh fruit is used, reduce the citric acid by ½tsp/3 grams.

❑ *If the honey has all been collected from one crop, the wine is likely to take on that characteristic, or you can add different flavours of your own choice.*

1

Borage and Malt

Golden Medium-Sweet Wine

2pts/1ltr borage leaves and flowers,
loosely packed (or 2oz/60g dried)
1lb/450g malt extract
2lb/900g sugar
1tsp/5g citric acid
½ tsp/3g tannin
1tsp/5g pectic enzyme
1tsp/5g yeast nutrient
Activated wine yeast, sherry type

(1) Rinse and coarsely chop up the flowers and leaves. **(2)** Drop them into 5 pints/2.85 litres of boiling water. Remove from the heat, cover, and leave to infuse overnight. **(3)** Heat the sugar and malt in 1½ pints/850 ml of boiling water, stirring constantly until dissolved. **(4)** Pour the sugar and malt syrup into a bucket, add the strained borage infusion, and stir well. When cool, 21°C (70°F), add the other ingredients and activated yeast. Cover closely and ferment for five days, stirring daily, then transfer to a 1 gallon/4.5 litre fermentation jar. Top up as necessary with cooled, boiled water, then fit a bored cork or bung, and airlock, and leave to ferment out. Rack when clear and stable, then bottle.

As a variation, 2-4 pints/1-2 litres of pure apple juice can be added to the must, but reduce the water accordingly. This will give the wine a slightly heavier body and modify the flavour a little.

Malt is not often used these days as an ingredient, but can be useful to give body to a wine.

1

2

This recipe makes a full-bodied wine with a delicious fresh flavour and scent.

4

3

Mint and Tea

Medium Dry Table Wine

1½pts/1ltr bruised mint leaves, or
1 level tblsp dried mint.
6pts/2.4ltrs hot tea
1lb/450g mixed dried fruit or
1pt/0.5ltr white grape concentrate
2lb/900g sugar
1tsp/5g citric acid
1tsp/5g pectic enzyme
1tsp/5g yeast nutrient
Activated wine yeast, sherry type

(1) Wash and chop up the dried fruit, and place this (or the grape concentrate if preferred) and the sugar into the initial fermentation vessel. **(2)** Add the washed and bruised mint leaves. Exclude all stalks. Prepare the 6 pints/2.4 litres of tea, and strain this into the bucket. Stir well with a wooden or plastic spoon to dissolve the sugar. When cool, 21°C (70°F), add the citric acid, pectic enzyme, yeast nutrient, and activated yeast. Cover and set aside to ferment for five days. **(3)** Strain into a 1 gallon glass fermentation jar. Top up if necessary with more must, obtained by washing the pulp with weak, lukewarm tea. Fit a bung and airlock, and leave to ferment to completion. Rack from the lees, and bottle when wine is mature and ready.

❑ *Different mint varieties produce differently flavoured wine. This recipe uses ordinary tea, but speciality teas can be used to gain additional flavour.*

1

2

3

1

2

Mandarin Orange

3 x 1lb/425g tins of mandarins in syrup

½pt/285ml white grape concentrate

1½lb/675g sugar

1tsp/5g citric acid

½tsp/3g tannin

1tsp/5g pectic enzyme

1tsp/5g yeast nutrient

Activated white wine yeast

3

4

(1) Place the fruit and syrup in a bucket, and mash the fruit by hand. Turn the sugar into a syrup by bringing it to the boil in 1 pint/0.5 litre of water; **(2)** add this to the fruit while still very hot. Add 4 pints/2.25 litres of cool water, and **(3)** when cool, the acid, nutrient, tannin and pectic enzyme Stir well, cover, and leave for twelve hours. In the meantime, activate the yeast in a starter bottle and leave in a warm place also for twelve hours. Pour the active yeast culture into the must and leave for two days, stirring at least once daily. **(4)** Strain off the solids, running the must into a demijohn, **(5)** add the grape concentrate, and **(6)** top up with water to the shoulder. Fit a bung and airlock, and leave the jar in a warm place, shaking it daily for the first few days. Allow the fermentation to reach completion, then place in a cool position to settle. Within a few days there will be a sediment in the bottom of the jar. Rack the wine off this into a clean demijohn, and add a crushed Campden tablet. Leave to settle again, racking when necessary. This wine is ready to drink in under a year.

This recipe makes an appetising, light, dry white wine, which can then be sweetened if desired with a non-fermenting sugar or sweetener.

❑ *Tins of broken mandarin segments are ideal for this recipe.*

5

6

Plum or Apricot

Most canned fruits are suitable for making into wine, particularly stoned fruits like plum and apricot. Use the recipe for Mandarin Wine, but substituting the chosen fruit. Red grape concentrate can be used instead of white, if a red wine is required. A good combination is red plums with white grape concentrate, making a pale rosé wine. As the acid level is always low in canned fruit, additional acid is an advantage. If fruit in natural juice (not syrup) is used, then the sugar can be increased to 2 pounds/900 grams The procedure is otherwise as above.

❑ ***Some people prefer to remove the stones from the must, to ensure the kernels do not flavour the wine.***

Balm and Rosehip

Light White Table Wine

4pts/2.25ltrs fresh balm leaves, or
2oz/60g dried leaves
6oz/175g dried rosehip shells
2 oranges and 2 lemons
2pts/1ltr preservative-free grapefruit juice
2¼ lb/1kg sugar
½ tsp/3g tannin or 1 cup of strong tea
1tsp/5g pectic enzyme
1tsp/5g yeast nutrient
Activated all-purpose wine yeast

(1) Rinse the leaves, and chop them coarsely. Place in 4 pints/2.25 litres of water, and bring to the boil. Turn off the heat, cover, and leave to infuse overnight. Dissolve the sugar in 2 pints/1 litre of hot water in the fermenting vessel. **(2)** Strain the liquor of the leaves into the bucket. **(3)** Add the rosehips and the grapefruit juice. Squeeze the juice from the oranges and lemons, and chop the zest (coloured skin, no white pith). When the bucket contents have cooled, add the juice, zest, additives and activated yeast. Cover and leave for five days, stirring daily. **(4)** Strain into a demijohn, and top up to the shoulder if necessary, with either cooled boiled water or fruit juice, and fit a bung and airlock. Leave to ferment out, and rack when clear.

This makes a pleasant, fragrant, light white wine. The leaves are best gathered in July when the plant is in flower.

❑ *Dried rosehips have the advantage over the fresh variety in that the risk of bitterness is greatly reduced.*

1

2

3

4

Rose Petal and grape concentrate

Medium Dry Rosé Wine

5pts/2.85ltrs pink and red rose

petals, or 2oz/60g dried petals

½ pint/285ml red grape concentrate

2lb/900g sugar

1tsp/5g mixed acids (citric, malic, tartaric)

½ tsp/3g tannin

1tsp/5g yeast nutrient

Activated wine yeast, Burgundy type

Activate the yeast in advance of making up the wine must. **(1)** Place the petals into the initial fermentation vessel together with the sugar and grape concentrate. Add six pints of hot water and stir well with a wooden or plastic spoon to dissolve the sugar. When cool, 21°C (70°F), add the remainder of the ingredients and the wine yeast.

Cover and set aside in a warm place to ferment for four days, pressing down the petals each day with a spoon. **(2)** Strain the liquor into a one gallon fermentation jar. Top up if necessary with apple juice. or cool, boiled water. Fit a bung and airlock, and leave to ferment out to completion. Rack from the lees when a sediment forms.

This wine can be imbibed while still fairly young, but improves with keeping for a few months. To make a white wine use white petals (and yellow if white petals are in short supply) and white grape concentrate; ½ pound/225 grams of sultanas or raisins may be used in lieu of the grape concentrate when making a white wine.

The water may be reduced by 1¾ pints/1 litre and a 1 litre carton of pure apple juice added instead. This gives a much improved wine, but one that will take a little longer to mature.

❏ *The petals can be collected daily, placed in a plastic bag, and frozen until you have enough to make the wine.*

1

2

1

Grape Juice and other Fruit Juices

6pts/3ltrs red or white grape juice
1lb/675g sugar
1tsp/5g citric acid
1tsp/5g pectic enzyme
1tsp/5g yeast nutrient
1 x 3mg vitamin B tablet
Activated wine yeast, to suit.

This wine can be red, white, or rosé, depending on the mixture of grape juice. This can be bought, generally in Tetrapaks, from supermarkets or grocery stores. Do check that they do not contain preservatives, as these will hinder the growth and activity of the yeast.

The sugar is converted to syrup by boiling it in 1 pint/0.5 litre of water, and cooling it. **(1)** It is then put directly into the demijohn, with all the other ingredients, and given a good swirling shake to mix the contents. **(2)** Add the activated yeast culture and sufficient

cooled, boiled water to bring the level up to the shoulder of the jar. Fit an airlock and bung. The must has to be kept in a warm place, and fermentation should start in about twelve hours. Shake the jar daily for the first week. When the fermentation has ended, put the jar in a cool spot, and leave it to settle.

After the first racking add a crushed Campden tablet. Rack again as and when a deposit forms.

This makes a very easy, everyday drinking wine; sweeten to taste with a non-fermenting sugar if required. It is ready to drink in about three months. Any other kind of fruit juice can be used, passion fruit, apple, grapefruit etc., either on their own or as a mixture.

With the stronger flavoured juices like grapefruit it is better to use 50 per cent of that juice and 50 per cent of apple juice.

❑ *Because of the short maturation time needed, this is a very good stop-gap wine when stocks are running low.*

2

Instant Coffee

Dry Table Wine

---

1 level tblsp instant coffee

½ lb/225g sultanas

2lb/900g sugar

1tsp/5g citric acid

1tsp/5g yeast nutrient

Activated wine yeast, all-purpose type

(1) Place the coffee, sugar, and citric acid into a bucket. **(2)** Chop the sultanas and add them, and then pour on 4 pints/2.25 litres of boiling water. Stir well, cover, and leave to cool. Add 3 pints/1.7 litres cool, boiled water, and the yeast culture and nutrient, cover, and stir daily for five days. **(3)** Then strain into the demijohn, top up to the bottom of the neck with water. **(4)** Fit bung and airlock and leave to ferment out. Rack, and bottle when stable in the usual way.

❑ *This makes a good substitute for iced coffee on a hot day.*

1

2

3

4

Autumn

Autumn is the period of rusts, golds, and deep reds. At this time of the year home wine making really comes into its own. It is the time of wild fruit in the hedgerows, which if looked at closely, become a mass of colour, ingredients, and interest, completely unnoticed by the passing motorist, but looked forward to with great enthusiasm by the wine maker. What lovelier way is there to spend a Sunday than in the countryside picking blackberries, with the whole family participating. Include a picnic hamper, a cool-box with a couple of bottles of last year's apple wine, garden chairs, and hopefully the sun shining, and what more could anyone ask for? The only drawback that this sort of day used to have was that on returning home it was imperative to use the collected fruit at once, before it started to spoil. This was sometimes quite a bore, as all you really wanted was to sit down and relax. Now many of us have freezers, and a quick rinse of the fruit is all that is needed before it is safely stored away. Fruit that has been frozen, even if only for a few days, tends to break down more easily, and the colour is extracted more quickly; for these reasons freezing is an advantage.

So what can we find in the hedgerows in September, October, and November?

There are of course the blackberries; there are still many miles of bramble hedges around. Two points to remember, though: do not pick too near a main road, as the diesel and petrol fumes do affect the fruit. And if you are deep in the country, do check that there has been no pesticide spraying recently. The berries should be really ripe for picking; a rule of thumb is that they are fully ripe if they pull off their husks easily. If they are not ripe your wine will have a 'woody' or 'green' flavour when finished.

Another inhabitant of the hedgerow is the wild rose; we have already used its petals, and now we have the bonus of its rosehips. Certain wild roses produce large, fleshy hips, like small crab apples. Hips are best picked after the first frost, which softens the outside skin. Care must be taken not to crush the pips as this causes bitterness in the wine. It is not recommended that you use an electric mixer for this fruit, it is much better to cut each hip in two, and then break them up with a wooden spoon or ladle.

Away from the bramble hedges are the larger boundaries, often containing elderberry bushes, again with a bonus to the winemaker. The elderflower gave us blossom for winemaking in the spring and early summer. In September and October the bushes are covered in bunches of small, black, shiny berries; in a really good year the whole bush can look black at a glance. The berry is about the size of a small blackcurrant, and grows in the shape of a flat-topped cluster

These need to be separated from their stalks before the wine can be made, and the best method of doing this is with a table fork. Again, it is important to pick the berries when they are fully ripe and to do this one has to battle with the local wild-bird population, as they, too, find elderberries very desirable. The biggest problem with elderberries is the excess tannin they contain, and there are several ways of dealing with this. The tannin is contained in the skins and stalks. As already mentioned, the berries should be removed from the stalks, and because of the high ratio of skins to juice, it is necessary to separate them as soon as

possible. You can either use one of the juice extraction methods, or leave the skins in the must for only a short time. It is important at the very beginning to decide what type of wine you are making. If it is to be a light wine that you will drink while it is still young, use the juice extraction method. If you are planning a richer, heavier wine, use the whole fruit, but the wine will have to be left longer to mature. The more tannin the wine contains, the longer the maturation period.

Sloes can also be found in the hedges, but are not always easily to spot. A far surer way of locating a potential crop is in the spring, when the bush, the blackthorn, is out in full bloom, often before the leaves appear. The splashes of white in an otherwise barren hedge are very easy to spot, and the site of the bush can be memorised for later in the year. Here again you and the birds are in opposition in the autumn, as the fully ripe fruit is a delicacy for them. Unfortunately, if you pick the sloes before they are ripe you will end up with a sour, bitter wine. As it is often late November before the sloes are ready to pick, there is a great temptation to hurry things along.

Apart from the sloe wine we can make, it is also possible to reproduce the well-known sloe gin. It is expensive but fun, and a recipe is included later.

1

2

Royal Elderberry

Heavy Sweet Red, Dessert-style

4lb/1.8kg fresh elderberries
1lb/450g chopped raisins
1lb/450g ripe bananas
1lb/450g dried dates
1kg can red grape concentrate
3lb/1.36kg sugar
1tsp/5g tartaric acid
½tsp/3g tannin
1tsp/5g pectic enzyme
1tsp/5g yeast nutrient
Activated wine yeast, Port style

(1) Place the elderberries in a large fermenting bucket with 2 pints/1 litre of boiling water. Chop the peeled bananas into chunks, and bring to the boil in 1 pint/500 ml of water. Simmer for 25 minutes, **(2)** and strain the 'gravy' into the bucket. Dissolve 2 pounds/900 grams of the sugar in 1 pint0.5 litre of boiling water and add this to the bucket. Put in the dried fruit (raisins and dates),

previously chopped, stir well and leave covered to cool. When the must is cool, add the grape concentrate and all else except the other 1 pound/450 grams of sugar and the yeast. The yeast is stirred in twelve hours later. Leave to ferment for four days, stirring twice daily, **(3)** then strain and place in a gallon jar. Top up if necessary, but leave ample space as there will be a lively fermentation. Fit a bung and airlock. As the fermentation slows down, convert the remaining sugar to a syrup by boiling it in ½ pint/280 ml of water for a couple of minutes, and leave it to cool. Add this a little at a time as the fermentation progresses, in this way the yeast will not be handicapped by a high sugar concentration in the must. A high alcohol level can be achieved by 'feeding' this way. **(4)** When the wine is finished, allow it to settle and clear, rack, and add a crushed Campden tablet. This wine needs at least two years to mature, and is definitely better for being left longer. The finishing gravity level should be about 1015, and this can be achieved by the addition of a small amount of sugar syrup. Stabilise the wine with a further Campden tablet and a teaspoonful of potassium sorbate.

❏ **The author has won several major awards with wine made from this recipe.**

3

4

Elderberry Regal Rosé

Dry Table Wine

2lb/900g fresh elderberries.

1lb/450g fully-ripe bananas

1lb/450g minced sultanas

2lb/900g sugar

½tsp/3g citric acid

1tsp/5g pectic enzyme

1tsp/5g yeast nutrient

Activated wine yeast, all-purpose or Burgundy type

Pour 2 pints/1 litre of boiling water over the elderberries and let them soak for 20 minutes, then crush the berries, squeeze, and strain off the liquid. **(1)** Put the elderberry liquor into the fermenting bucket with the minced sultanas and add 2 pints/1 litre of boiling water. Dissolve the sugar in 1 pint/0.5 litre of water, bring to the boil, and add it to the must. Chop the peeled bananas into chunks, bring them to the boil in 1 pint/0.5 litre of water and simmer for 25 minutes. **(2)** Strain off the banana 'gravy' and add it to the must. When cooled to about 21°C (70°F) add the acid, yeast nutrient, pectic enzyme and the activated yeast. Cover and leave to ferment for three days, stirring twice daily, then strain and transfer to a demijohn. Top the jar up to the shoulder with cool, boiled water, and fit airlock and bung. Leave to ferment to completion. Rack as necessary until the wine falls clear.

❑ ***This wine is ready to drink in a year, and is best served chilled.***

Sloe Gin

8oz/250g ripe sloes

4-6oz/125-175g sugar

14floz/350ml gin

Remove any stalks from the sloes and wash the fruit. Prick the sloes at both ends to release their juice and put them into a screw-top container, which should be no more than half full. Add the sugar to taste and top up with the gin. Seal the container and shake it vigorously.

Repeat the shaking process twice a day for two to four weeks after which time the sloes will have turned the liquid a rich, red colour. The liqueur should now be left to mature. Although the sloe gin is ready to drink after a few weeks, it improves if left for a year or more. If desired, after three months the liquid may be strained off and bottled before being left to finish maturing.

1

2

Sloe, Sultana and Grape Juice

Claret-style Dry Red Table Wine (5 gallons/22.5 litres)

12lb/5.4kg fresh sloes
4lb/1.8kg sultanas
4lb/1.8kg honey
4pts/2.25ltrs red grape concentrate
3tsp/15g yeast nutrient
3tsp/15g pectic enzyme
Bordeaux yeast starter culture

If you can foil the birds, leave the sloes on the bush as long as possible to minimise the acid content.

Wash the sloes and stone them if possible, **(1)** crush the fruit and mix it with the chopped sultanas in a sterile bucket. **(2)** Add the honey, nutrient, and 3 gallons/13.5 litres of boiling water, cover and leave. When cool, add the yeast starter and ferment on the pulp for two to three days, **(3)** then strain and press lightly. Add the grape concentrate and sufficient water to bring the volume up to 4.5 gallons/20 litres. **(4)** Thereafter continue in the normal way, fermenting the wine under airlock; it can be split among five demijohns if you do not have one container large enough. Follow the general principles outlined above for blackberry wine. When fermentation is complete, rack and add three crushed Campden tablets. Store for long maturation, in a cask if at all possible. Protect from light to save the colour deteriorating.

❑ *This wine needs a long maturing period, and is best kept in a cask.*

1

2

3

4

Crabapple

Dry to Medium White Table Wine

5-6lbs/2-3kg crabapples
½pt/280ml white grape concentrate
¼tsp/1g tannin
1tsp/5g mixed citric and tartaric acid
1tsp/5g pectic enzyme
2lb/1.1kg granulated white sugar
1tsp/5g yeast nutrient
Bordeaux white wine yeast

Activate the yeast in advance. **(1)** Place the sugar and grape concentrate together with the chopped, pulped, or grated apples into the initial fermentation vessel, including the skins and cores. Pour in 6 pints/3 litres of warm water, **(2)** and stir well to dissolve the sugar and the grape concentrate. When cool, 20°C (70°F), add the remainder of the ingredients. Cover and set aside in a warm place to ferment for seven days, **(3)** then strain into a glass 1 gallon fermentation jar through a nylon sieve placed over a large funnel. Top up with cooled, boiled water, using this to wash the pulp. Fit the bung and airlock and leave the must to ferment out to completion. Rack from the lees when the wine has fallen star-bright.

This wine benefits from chilling before serving. A stronger and social wine can be obtained by adding 8 ounces/225 grams of light malt extract. A litre of pure apple juice can be substituted for a litre of water at the outset.

❏ *Whilst collecting the crab apples, why not collect a few extra and make some crab apple jelly?*

1

2

3

1

2

Blackberry

Dry Red Table Wine

4lb/1.8kg blackberries
2lb/900g sugar
1tsp/5g pectic enzyme
1tsp/5g citric acid
1tsp/5g yeast nutrient
All purpose yeast

Pick and wash the blackberries; these can be stored in the freezer until required. **(1)** Place the (thawed) fruit in a white bucket; **(2)** pour onto the fruit 4 pints/ 2.25 litres of boiling water. Convert the sugar to a syrup by bringing it to the boil with 1 pint/0.5 litre of water; this makes 2 pints/1 litre of syrup. At this stage you have 4 pints/2.25 litres of water plus 2 pints/1 litre of syrup, plus an unknown quantity of juice from the fruit. This is why you do not add 8 pints/4.5 litres of water at the beginning, to make the

gallon of wine. Activate the yeast by making a starter bottle, placing the yeast and a teaspoon of sugar in ¼ pint/140 ml of lukewarm water. Plug the jar or bottle with a wad of un-medicated cotton wool; small bubbles will appear in a few hours to a day, depending on the yeast.

When the contents of the bucket have cooled to about 20°C (70°F), **(3)** add the other ingredients and the **(4)** yeast starter. Leave for four days, stirring daily. During this time the yeast will extract the juice and colour from the fruit. The must will become frothy, and a 'cap' of fruit will form. The daily stirring is to break up this cap.

Next strain the must off using a sieve or nylon bag through a funnel into a demijohn or glass fermentation jar. Top up to the shoulder with cooled, boiled water or apple juice if necessary. Fit a bung and airlock, and place the jar in a warm place. The time the must takes to ferment to dryness, in othe words to convert the sugar to alcohol and carbon dioxide, depends on the temperature and conditions. It is beneficial to shake the jar daily for the first few days to prevent the yeast settling as a sediment.

When there are no more bubbles coming through the airlock, the wine will taste very dry; leave it to settle for a few days. Rack the wine into another demijohn, add a crushed Campden tablet to reduce the chances of further fermentation, and refit the airlock. Now leave it in a cool place to settle. During the next few days the wine will gradually clear, forming another sediment. Do not allow the wine to 'sit' on this for long as it will give the wine a yeasty taste. Rack whenever a sediment forms, but add another Campden tablet only after the last racking. Keep the demijohn topped up to the shoulder with cooled, boiled water, to avoid the risk of oxidation. When you are finally satisfied with the wine's clarity, and are sure that there is no longer any fermentation, close the jar with a cork or safety closure and put it away in a cool place for the wine to mature for at least a year. If you have to use a rubber closure, place a piece of cling film between the rubber and the wine, to prevent the wine picking up the taste of the rubber, and the bung in time welding itself to the neck of the jar.

❑ *Surely one of the most popular ingredients for home-made wine, and picking the fruit can be fun too.*

3

4

Rosehip

Medium Sweet Social Wine

2lb/900g fresh rose hips
3lb/1.35kg sugar
1tsp/5g pectic enzyme
1tsp/5g citric acid
1tsp/5g yeast nutrient
All purpose yeast

(1) Wash the hips well, then cut them in half or crush them with a piece of wood or a mallet. Put the sugar in a clean bucket with the rose hips, and pour over them 6 pints/3 litres of boiling water. Stir well to dissolve the sugar. When the liquor has cooled to 20°C (70°F), add the rest of the ingredients and the yeast starter. Leave in a warm place for a week, covered closely, and stir daily.
(2) Then strain through a jelly bag, sieve, or piece of nylon netting stretched over a large funnel, into a fermentation jar.
(3) Fit a bung and airlock. When, after about three months, the wine clears, rack it into a fresh jar, add a crushed Campden tablet, and leave for a further three months before racking again and bottling.

Altogether this is a very busy time of the year for for the winemaker, as there is an abundance of fresh ingredients around. For those less energetic amongst us there is still a wide range of dried ingredients that can be used This section of the chapter concentrates on the dried grains, and fruits such as rice, wheat, and prunes, from all of which one can produce a first-class wine. However, it also shows that it is very easy to blend both dried and fresh materials together to obtain a different style. One example used is potato and wheat 'whisky', possibly one of the oldest and best known of all the original home-made wine recipes. Over the years, with the progress of the hobby, this recipe has become more sophisticated and better balanced, but it is still basically a strong drink.

❏ *Do not process them in an electric mixer as this will break the seeds and release the bitterness.*

2

3

Rice and Raisin

A quick and easy table wine

| 2lb/900g raisins |
| 2lb/900g rice |
| 2lb/900g sugar |
| Juice of 1 orange and 1 lemon, medium size |
| General purpose yeast. |
| Water to 1gal/4.5ltr total |

Dissolve the sugar by bringing it to the boil in 1 pint/0.5 litre of water. Allow it to cool, and pour it over the rice and raisins (do not chop or mince the raisins) in a bucket. **(1)** Then add the juice, a further 6 pints/3 litres of cool water, and sprinkle on or stir in the yeast. **(2)** Stir and leave in a warm place. Stir daily for fourteen days, **(3)** then strain through muslin into a 1 gallon/4.5 litre jar. Top up with cooled, boiled water and fit a bung and airlock. Keep in a warm place until fermentation stops, then filter the wine through one of the simple popular filters that are commercially available, or through coarse filter paper, and the wine is then ready for drinking straight away. If not drunk within two months, add a crushed Campden tablet, and the wine can then be left for up to about nine months.

❏ *A recipe that is very useful if a party is pending and time is short.*

1

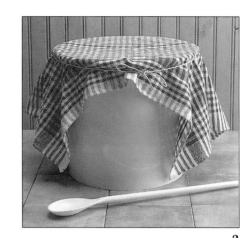

2

3

Wheat and Raisin

1lb/675g wheat
2lb/900g granulated white sugar
½lb/225g raisins
1 lemon and 1 orange
½tsp/3g ground ginger
½ cup cold strong tea
1tsp/5g pectic enzyme
1tsp/5g yeast nutrient
All purpose wine yeast

1

(1) Put the wheat in a large saucepan or preserving pan with 4 pints/2.25 litres of water and bring to the boil. Simmer for half an hour, then strain the liquid into a plastic bucket. **(2)** Add the sugar, the zest (no pith) and juice of the lemon and orange, the chopped raisins and the ginger. Pour in the tea, and stir well with a plastic spoon to dissolve the sugar. When the mixture is lukewarm, add the pectic enzyme and leave covered in a warm place for twenty-four hours. Then stir in the yeast and yeast nutrient. Cover the bucket and leave it for eight days, stirring it occasionally and watching that the room it is in remains comfortably warm. After this period, strain it into a demijohn, fit a bung and airlock and leave to ferment out. Rack into another demijohn and allow the wine to clear fully before bottling. This wine may need several rackings before it clears, but be patient, it is worth it in the end. Keep it to mature for at least six months – much longer if possible.

❑ *The wheat can be crushed, allowing the husk to soften more quickly.*

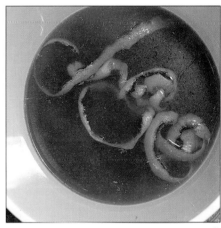

2

Wheat Whiskey

A strong, dryish wine, that can be sweetened slightly

1pt/0.5ltr wheat
2lb/900g sultanas, minced or chopped
2 large potatoes, finely grated.
2lb/900g demerara sugar
Grated rind (zest) and juice of two lemons
½ cup cold tea
1tsp/5g pectic enzyme
1tsp/5g yeast nutrient
All purpose yeast

Peel and grate the potatoes. **(1)** Mix in a plastic bucket with the pint of wheat, sultanas, sugar, zest and juice of the lemons, tea and pectic enzyme. Pour on 6 pints/3 litres of tepid water and mix very thoroughly with a plastic spoon. Leave covered for twenty-four hours, then stir in the yeast and yeast nutrient. Re-cover the bucket, and stand for ten to fourteen days in the warmth, stirring daily. Strain off the wine carefully into a demijohn and fit a bung and airlock. Keep warm and let fermentation continue until complete. When the wine starts to clear from the surface, rack and add a crushed Campden tablet. Rack again when a sediment forms and the wine is quite clear. Mature for at least three months, longer if possible, before bottling.

❑ *A powerful brew, and one on which can be laid the blame for many of the past legends of winemaking.*

1

Maize

Medium Dry White Table Wine

2lb/900g flaked maize (available from homebrew and health food shops)
2lb/1.1kg demerara sugar
2pts/1ltr unsweetened fresh orange juice
1lb/450g sultanas, chopped
2lb/900g sugar
1tsp/5g tartaric acid
1tsp/5g yeast nutrient
All purpose yeast

Activate the yeast in a starter bottle. Soak the maize overnight in the fermenting bucket with 2 pints/1 litre of water. **(1)** Dissolve the sugar in a pan with 2 pints/1 litre of boiling water, and leave to cool. Place the sugar syrup, all the rest of the ingredients, and the activated yeast into the bucket with a further 2 pints/1 litre of cooled, boiled water, and stir well. Cover, and leave in a warm place for five days stirring daily. Strain into a demijohn without pressing the pulp, top up to the shoulder with more water, and fit a bung and airlock, and leave to ferment out. When the wine clears, rack it from the sediment and add a crushed Campden tablet. If it has fermented to dryness, add a little non-fermenting sweetener to bring it back to a medium sweet wine. This is very nice when served chilled.

❑ ***This is for the winemaker who likes to try new wines.***

1

Prune

3lb/1.36kg prunes
½lb/225g chopped raisins
2pts/1ltr red grape juice
2lb/900g sugar
1tsp/5g pectic enzyme
1tsp/5g citric acid
1tsp/5g yeast nutrient
Burgundy yeast

Activate the yeast in a starter bottle. Prepare the prunes by soaking them for twenty-four hours in a bowl of cold tea. Make sure they are just covered, and stir them frequently. **(1)** Next day strain off and discard the liquid, placing the prunes in a fermentation bucket. Squeeze them by hand to loosen and remove the stones. Add the raisins and 3 pints/1.5 litres of boiling water. Dissolve the sugar in a further 2 pints/1 litre of boiling water, and add this to the must. When cooled to 20°C (70°F) add the grape juice and additives. After twelve hours add the activated yeast. Leave covered in a warm place to ferment for three days, stirring twice daily. Then strain out the solids, pouring the liquid into a demijohn, top up to the shoulder if necessary, fit a bung and airlock, and leave to ferment out. Rack when finished, adding a crushed Campden tablet, and rack again if a sediment forms as the wine clears.

❑ *This wine is ready to drink in nine months and is best left as a medium or sweet wine.*

1

coconut

Medium White Wine

1lb/450g desiccated coconut

1lb/450g rice

1lb/450g chopped dates

3lb/1.36kg granulated white sugar

1tsp/5g citric acid

1tsp/5g yeast nutrient

Selected wine yeast, Sauternes preferably

Activate the wine yeast beforehand.
(1) Put the rice in a large saucepan with 6 pints/3 litres of water, bring it to the boil, **(2)** and simmer for three minutes. In the meantime, chop the dates and put them and the coconut into a separate pan. Strain the rice water on to them and boil for fifteen minutes. Strain this liquor onto the sugar and yeast nutrient, and stir well to dissolve them. Allow to cool to 20°C (70°F), then add the yeast starter. **(3)** Pour the must into a fermenting jar up to the level of the shoulder, fit a bung and airlock and leave to ferment in a warm place. Keep the small surplus must in a separate bottle. When the initial frothy fermentation has died down after a few days, top up to the shoulder with the surplus must, refit the airlock, and leave to ferment. Rack after three months, and rack again after another three months, adding a crushed Campden tablet. Store for one year, sweeten to taste with a non-fermenting sweetener, and serve slightly chilled.

❑ *Be sure to plug this well with cotton wool to keep out bacteria etc., but don't seal it completely.*

1

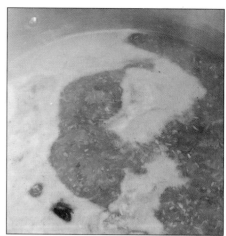

2

3

Winter

If you have, as suggested in previous chapters, taken advantage of the autumn hedgerows laden with elderberries, blackberries and sloes, it is quite possible that as winter comes round the freezer is groaning with the weight of the fruits stored. Just as squirrels store acorns to help them survive this season, so we can make sure we do not run short of the essentials for winemaking. The other easily obtained ingredients during this time are vegetables, which, if you grow them yourself, provide a very cheap source of winemaking material. Alternatively, a visit to a local market can supply you with the necessary produce at very little expense.

At different times of the year the parsnip can be used to make various styles of wine. When young, parsnips make a light wine with sufficient body to be a dry table wine. But leave the roots in the ground until after a frost or two, and a very different wine is the result. This will tend towards an aperitif style, with a clean, full, earthy bite to it; if left to oxidize to a small degree, and fed with sufficient sugar to produce the required alcohol, it can imitate a sherry. All types of 'sherry' can be made by varying the amount of sweetness and alcohol of the end product. The carrot, too, has the same traits. The young roots are much sweeter than those left in the ground for some time, but it is the latter which make the better wines.

With all vegetables, the method is the same. The roots are washed and scrubbed, but not peeled. They are then cut up and boiled until tender and the water, or 'gravy' as it is known, is drained off; it is only this gravy that is used for winemaking. Take care not to add salt in this initial stage of boiling; one lady of the author's acquaintance finished up with a well-salted gallon of wine. The vegetable solids can be stored or frozen, to become part of Sunday lunch or some other meal when salted and reheated. If the flavour of your finished wine is rather more earthy or oxidized than you enjoy – this does occasionally happen, especially with beetroot wine – try heating some with the addition of a little spice and sugar. The author once suggested this to an elderly gentleman who had such a problem with a beetroot wine; he made himself two hot toddies every night, and told her later that he slept better that winter than he had for years!

If you are not fortunate enough to have the freezer full of vegetables, or to grow your own, this is still the time of year to make your wine. Dried fruit, available throughout the year, is more prominently displayed during the pre-Christmas period, and a varied selection is to be had. Some manufacturers coat the fruit with a film of liquid paraffin, so it is advisable to wash all dried fruit in warm water before use; the paraffin will otherwise inhibit the wine fermentation. The use of dried fruit is covered more fully in the spring section.

Celery

White Table Wine

3lb/1.36kg celery
½lb/225g chopped sultanas
2lb/900g granulated white sugar
1tsp/5g citric acid
1tsp/5g yeast nutrient
1tsp/5g pectic enzyme
½tsp/3g grape tannin
Sachet of yeast for a white wine

1

2

(1) Wash and scrub the celery and chop it in short lengths, into a large saucepan. Cover with unsalted cold water, bring to the boil, and simmer for about twenty minutes, until the celery is soft but not to the point of mashing. **(2)** Strain off the cooled liquid into a clean demijohn, add the sugar as a syrup, and top up with cold, boiled water to the shoulder of the jar. Add the acid, nutrient and enzyme, fit an airlock, and leave for twenty-four hours in a warm place. Then add the yeast culture, refit the airlock, and leave to ferment in a warm place, shaking daily.

When the wine begins to clear, leave it to settle, and rack as soon as necessary, adding a crushed Campden tablet and topping up with cool, boiled water. Rack again after six months, or sooner if necessary. This makes a lovely, light-coloured wine, and looks very attractive, especially if filtered and polished. It should be dry, but can easily be sweetened up with the addition of some white grape concentrate.

❑ *The celery need not be wasted, but can be used as a vegetable.*

Carrot

Dry White Table Wine

4lb/1.8kg carrots – not new crop

1pt/500ml (can) white grape concentrate

2lb/900g granulated white sugar

1tsp/5g citric acid

1tsp/5g yeast nutrient

1tsp/5g pectic enzyme

½tsp/3g grape tannin

1 x 3mg vitamin B compound tablet

Sachet of yeast for a white wine

Activate the yeast in a starter bottle. **(1)** Wash, scrub and slice the carrots, and bring to the boil in sufficient water to cover them, simmering for twenty minutes, or until tender, **(2)** and strain the liquid into a fermenting bucket, discarding the carrot pulp. Add the sugar to the hot liquid in the bucket, and stir well to dissolve it. Leave to cool to about 20°C (70°F), then stir in the grape concentrate and other ingredients except the yeast. Cover and leave in the warm for twenty-four hours. Add the activated yeast, and ferment for two days before pouring it into a clean demijohn. Top up to the shoulder with cooled, boiled water, fit a bung and airlock and leave to ferment to dryness, which may be in about fifteen days. Move to a cooler situation, and allow to clear and settle, racking as soon as a sediment appears. Rack again as necessary, topping up each time with apple juice. This produces a dry white table wine of very good quality, drinkable after six to nine months.

If a sweet social wine is required, increase the quantity of carrots and grape concentrate, and add half a pound of chopped raisins to the bucket initially. Leave the must in the bucket for a week to allow the yeast to extract the goodness from the raisins, then strain it into the demijohn and continue as before. The fermentation will take a little longer.

❑ ***The author first met this dessert carrot wine while judging near Southampton, gave it a first prize, and was amazed when she learned what the main ingredient was.***

1

2

Potato

Sweet Social Wine

6lb/2.7kg old potatoes
2½-3lb/1.1-1.36kg sugar; demerara can be used to produce a golden wine with a fuller flavour
1tsp/5g citric acid
1tsp/5g yeast nutrient
1tsp/5g pectic enzyme
1tsp/5g Amylozyme or Diastase starch-reducing enzyme
½tsp/3g grape tannin, or a cup of strong cold tea
Sachet of yeast for a white wine

Wash and scrub the unpeeled potatoes, and slice thinly into a large saucepan. **(1)** Cover with unsalted cold water, bring to the boil and simmer for about twenty minutes, until the potatoes are soft, but not to the point of mashing. **(2)** Strain off the cooled liquid into a clean demijohn, **(3)** add the sugar as a syrup, and top up with cold, boiled water to the shoulder of the jar. Add the acid, nutrient, and enzyme, fit an airlock, and leave for twenty-four hours in a warm place. Then add the yeast culture, refit the airlock, and leave to ferment in a warm place, shaking daily.

When the wine starts to clear, leave it to settle, and rack as soon as necessary, adding a crushed Campden tablet and topping up with cool, boiled water. Rack again after six months, or sooner if necessary. This wine needs at least eighteen months to two years to mature, and can then be sweetened to suit your palate, either with white grape concentrate or a non-fermentable sweetener.

❏ *The maturation period is important, as this wine improves greatly with keeping. It is interesting to compare a bottle from an old batch with one from a recent fermentation.*

1

2

Aperitif Dry White

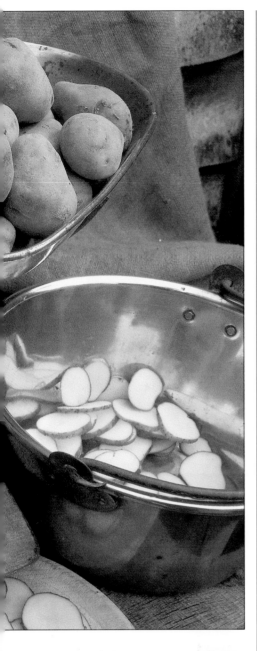

1½ lb/675g parsnips
1½ lb/675g turnips
1½ lb/675g carrots
2 lb/900g granulated white sugar
1 tsp/5g citric acid
1 tsp/5g yeast nutrient
1 tsp/5g pectic enzyme
½ tsp/3g grape tannin
Sachet of wine yeast

Make a starter bottle with the yeast to activate it. **(1)** Wash and scrub all the vegetables and slice them thinly into a large pan. Cover with cold water. Bring to the boil and simmer for about twenty minutes, until the vegetables are soft, but not to the point of mashing. Strain off the solids and let the liquid cool. Dissolve the sugar in 1 pint/0.5 litre of boiling water, and let this cool also. Add the vegetable liquor and the sugar syrup to a sterilised demijohn, and top up to the shoulder of the jar with cool, boiled water, then swirl round thoroughly to mix the contents. Add the acid, nutrient, tannin and enzyme, fit a bung and airlock, and leave for twenty-four hours in a warm place. Then add the yeast, refit the airlock, and leave to ferment in a warm place, shaking daily for the first few days. When the wine begins to clear, leave it to settle and rack off the sediment as soon as necessary, adding one crushed Campden tablet afterwards. Rack again after six months and top up, or sooner if a thick sediment appears.

❏ *The wine should be light in character, and dry, and is drinkable after ten months. It can be allowed to become slightly oxidised.*

3

1

Beetroot

Dry Red Table Wine

3lb/1.36kg beetroot

2lb/1.1kg white granulated sugar

3 medium-sized oranges

4-6 cloves, according to strength of flavour preferred

1tsp/5g tartaric acid

1tsp/5g pectic enzyme

1tsp/5g yeast nutrient

1 sachet all-purpose yeast

Use young beetroot if possible, as they do not have the earthiness of older roots. Wash the beetroot well, but do not peel. Cut into thin slices and put in a saucepan or preserving pan with 5 pints/2.5 litres water. Bring to the boil and simmer until the beetroot is just tender. Strain off the liquid, and put aside the beetroot for culinary use. Return liquid to the saucepan and add the juice and zest (no pith) of the fruit, the sugar and the cloves. Heat just enough to dissolve the sugar, stirring all the time. Let the liquid cool right down, then pour it into a sterile plastic bucket. Add a crushed Campden tablet and the pectic enzyme, and leave covered in warm surroundings for twenty-four hours. Add the yeast and yeast nutrient, cover the bucket carefully and leave for three days, stirring daily. Strain the wine into a demijohn, top up to the shoulder with cool, boiled water, fit a bung and airlock and ferment until dry. When fermentation has finished, rack the young wine into another demijohn to clear, and rack again as necessary.

This wine can be ready to drink in six months; it will lose some of its deep red colour and become tawny if left.

❏ *It is one of the most suitable to use for mulled wine or a hot toddy.*

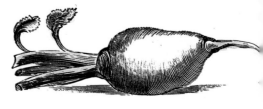

1

2

Parsnip

Dry Sherry-style Wine

3lb/1.36kg parsnips
½pt/280ml white grape concentrate
2½lb/1.1kg granulated white sugar
2tsp/10g citric acid
1tsp/5g pectic enzyme
1tsp/5g yeast nutrient
½tsp/3g grape tannin
1 x 3mg vitamin B tablet
1 sachet all purpose yeast

Make up a starter bottle to activate the yeast. Simmer the washed and sliced parsnips for ten minutes in sufficient unsalted water to cover them; **(1)** strain the liquor into a white plastic bucket, **(2)** cover, and leave to cool to room temperature. **(3)** Stir into the cooled liquor the crushed Campden tablet and pectic enzyme, cover again and leave for twenty-four hours. **(4)** Dissolve the sugar in 1 pint/0.5 litre of boiling water and add it to the parsnip liquor. **(5)** Put in the grape concentrate and other additives, and add 2 pints/1 litre of cold water. When cooled to 21°C (70°F), add the yeast culture. **(6)** Fit a bung and airlock and maintain the temperature. After ten days top up to the shoulder, if necessary, with water of the same temperature and refit the airlock. When the fermentation appears to have stopped – no bubbles passing through the airlock, starting to clear from the surface downwards – take a hydrometer reading. When this is below 1000, and remains static at three-day intervals, syphon the wine from the deposit into another clean and sterile demijohn. Top up with water at 21°C (70°F), refit the airlock and maintain the temperature until the wine clears. Rack into a clean jar, add a crushed Campden tablet, and keep for at least twelve months before bottling and drinking.

❑ *If you want the wine to oxidise, like sherry, plug the demijohn with cotton wool instead of fitting the airlock.*

3

4

5

6

Dried fruits are useful for wine making in winter, when fresh ingredients are far fewer.

Dried Fruit

A Full, Sweet, Red Dessert Wine

1lb/450g sultanas
1lb/450g raisins
1lb/450g dried elderberries
½lb/225g dates
½lb/225g dried bananas
2lb/1kg can red grape concentrate
3lb/1.36kg granulated white sugar
1tsp/5g citric acid
1tsp/5g yeast nutrient
1tsp/5g pectic enzyme
Sachet of Sauternes yeast

Activate the yeast in a starter bottle. Convert the sugar to syrup by boiling it in 1 pint/0.5 litre of water, and leave it to cool. Store it in a stoppered container. **(1)** Wash, rough dry and chop all the dried ingredients, **(2)** place them in a fermentation bucket, and pour over them 5 pints/2.5 litres of boiling water. Stir well, cover, and leave for twenty-four hours, stirring twice more during this time. Then put in the grape juice, additives, 1 pint/0.5 litre of sugar syrup, and the yeast culture, cover and leave for four days for the fermentation to begin, stirring at least once a day. Strain the liquid from the pulp to a demijohn (see note below). Fit an airlock, and stand the demijohn in a warm place and leave to ferment, shaking daily. As the fermentation dies down, add more sugar syrup, about five fluid ounces, or ¼ pint/ 140 ml, until either all the sugar is used or the fermentation ceases. Leave to settle, and rack when a sediment is formed. This wine will take a long time to mature, and is best left in the demijohn rather than being bottled. It is advisable to top up after racking with either grape concentrate or a fruit juice, so as not to dilute the wine.

1

❏ *The pulp can be used to make 1 gallon/4.5 litres of table wine by returning it to the bucket and adding an extra 2 pounds/900 grams of sugar as cooled syrup, more cool water, 1 teaspoon/5 grams each of acid and of nutrient, and straining it into a fresh demijohn after five days. Ferment out to dry and rack in the usual manner.*

2

Ginger

Medium Dry White Wine

2oz/75g fresh root ginger
1lb/450g chopped sultanas
2lb/900g bananas
2lb/1.1kg granulated white sugar
1tsp/5g citric acid
1tsp/5g yeast nutrient
1tsp/5g pectic enzyme
Sachet of yeast for a white wine

Activate the yeast in a starter bottle. **(1)** Break the root ginger into pieces, and put it with the chopped sultanas and sugar into a fermentation bucket. Pour on 5 pints/2.8 litres of boiling water, and stir well to dissolve the sugar. Peel and chop the bananas into small pieces and boil them in a pint of water for twenty minutes, **(2)** then strain the liquid into the bucket. When cooled to 20°C (70°F), add the rest of the ingredients and the yeast culture and cover the bucket. Ferment for four days in a warm place, stirring twice daily, then strain the liquid into a demijohn. Fit an airlock, and leave to ferment in the warm. Rack four weeks later, by which time the fermentation should have stopped. Add a crushed Campden tablet, top up with water, and refit the airlock. Rack again in about six months. This wine is drinkable at that time and is excellent as a 'hot toddy'.

❑ *A wine that definitely takes on the characteristics of the ingredient, and is very popular with people who like the flavour of ginger.*

1

2

Gooseberry and Sultana

Medium Dry White Wine

1 x 14oz/415g tin of gooseberries
1lb/450g chopped sultanas
2 large juicy oranges or lemons
½ pint/280ml white grape juice concentrate
¼oz/10g (about a dessertspoon) of dried elderflower florets
1lb/675g granulated white sugar
1tsp/5g mixed citric and malic acid
1tsp/5g yeast nutrient
1tsp/5g pectic enzyme
½tsp/3g grape tannin
Sachet of yeast for a white wine, Riesling suggested

(1) Make up a starter bottle to activate the yeast. Rinse the sultanas in warm water, drain, and dry on a cloth. Chop (a 'chipping' cutter is useful), **(2)** and place them into the initial fermentation vessel with the gooseberries, their juice and the sugar. **(3)** Add the citrus fruit juice and zest (peel minus the white pith), the elderflower florets, and the grape concentrate. **(4)** Pour in 5 pints/2.8 litres of hot water and stir well with a plastic spoon. Cover, and when cooled to **(5)** 21°C (70°F), add the tannin, acid, pectic enzyme, yeast nutrient and the activated wine yeast. **(6)** Cover, and set aside in the warm to ferment for seven days, stirring daily, **(7)** then strain the liquid into a 1 gallon 4.5 litre fermentation jar (demijohn). Use a nylon sieve placed over a funnel. Top up as necessary to the shoulder of the jar, using cool water 'washed' through the pulp in the sieve. Fit an airlock, and leave to ferment to completion.

In due course, when there is a thick sediment, rack, and add a crushed Campden tablet. Leave to clear, rack again, and drink when ready. At least three months maturation should be allowed.

1

2

❑ *The use of canned fruit, pure concentrated fruit juices and dried florets will enable production to take place all the year round, but fresh ingredients may be substituted when they are available.*

3

4

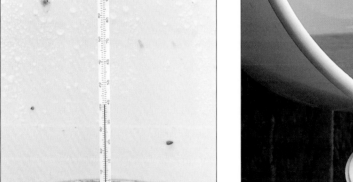

5

6

7

Date

Medium Sweet Wine

2lb/900g dates, sliced

½pint/280ml white grape concentrate

1lb/450g granulated white sugar

1tsp/5g citric acid

1tsp/5g yeast nutrient

2tsp/10g pectic enzyme

1 x 3mg vitamin B compound tablet

Sachet of yeast for a white wine

Activate the yeast beforehand. **(1)** Place the dates and sugar in a plastic bucket, and pour 4 pints/2.25 litres of boiling water over them, stirring until the sugar is dissolved, then cover. When down to room temperature, add the remaining ingredients and the yeast, and cover again. **(2)** Ferment on the pulp for four days, stirring the cap beneath the surface twice daily. **(3)** Strain off into a demijohn, add the grape concentrate, and top up to the shoulder with cool, boiled water. Fit a bung and airlock, and leave to ferment at 21°C (70°F) until dry. Rack into a clean jar, top up with water and a crushed Campden tablet, and refit the airlock. If a heavy pulp has formed after ten days, rack and top up again. Mature in a cool place and rack after six months. It will probably be drinkable at this time, but will improve for at least another year.

❑ *This is normally a medium sweet wine, but the sweetness can be adjusted to taste.*

Fig and Bananas

Sweet Golden Social Wine

2lb/900g dried figs, thinly sliced
8oz/225g dried bananas, thinly sliced
3oz/100g raisins, chopped
2lb/900g granulated white sugar
2 medium sized juicy lemons
1tsp/5g yeast nutrient
1tsp/5g pectic enzyme
Sachet of wine yeast

Activate the yeast in a starter bottle. Dissolve the sugar in 1 pint/0.5 litre of boiling water. **(1)** Place all the dried ingredients into a large bowl or fermentation bucket, and pour over them 4 pints/2.25 litres of boiling water. Stir vigorously, cover, then leave for twenty-four hours, stirring occasionally. **(2)** Add the cooled sugar syrup, and the zest and juice of the lemons, making sure no white pith is used. **(3)** The additives and the yeast culture can also be added. **(4)** Cover the vessel and leave to ferment for four days, stirring twice daily. Then strain off the liquid into a demijohn, top up with tepid, boiled water, and fit an airlock. Leave to ferment in a warm place, shaking daily.

When the wine starts to clear, leave it to settle, and rack off when a sediment has formed. Top up, and add a crushed Campden tablet. Rack again after six months, or when necessary because a sediment forms, until the wine is clear and bright. Sweeten to your personal taste.

To make a dessert wine successfully, some people say you need 20 pounds/9 kilos of fruit just to make 1 gallon/4.5 litres. One way to achieve this is to use dried fruit, where one measure is equal to four measures of fresh fruit. It is important when using dried fruit to wash it well in warm water to remove the oily or sulphurous substances used in packaging. Despite the seemingly large amount of fruit in the following recipe, it is to make 1 gallon/4.5 litres of dessert wine.

❏ *This is the very first wine the author ever made, and it won her the Petrose Trophy for Novice of the Year at Poole Wine Circle. It is still used for demonstration purposes.*

1

3

1

2

3

4

Dried Bilberries and Elderberries

Dry Red Table Wine

½lb/225g dried bilberries

½lb/225g dried elderberries

½lb/225g raisins, washed and chopped

2lb/900g granulated white sugar

1tsp/5g citric acid

1tsp/5g yeast nutrient

1tsp/5g pectic enzyme

Sachet of yeast for a red wine

Activate the wine yeast. Rinse the bilberries and elderberries, drain them, and then cover with 5 pints/2.8 litres of boiling water. Add the raisins, sugar, acid, and yeast nutrient and stir well to dissolve the sugar. When cool, add the pectic enzyme and yeast starter. Cover, and ferment on the pulp for two days, then strain off the liquid into a clean demijohn. Make up to 1 gallon/4.5 litres with cool water and fit a bung and airlock. Leave to ferment in a warm place and rack when a thick sediment forms, topping up with water or apple juice. When clear and stable, rack again and add a crushed Campden tablet. This wine needs to mature for at least twelve months.

❏ *It is more successful when made with fresh fruit, but this is a very good substitute.*

Barley Wine

Dry White Wine

1lb/450g barley
¼tsp/2g ground ginger
1 lemon
1 orange
½lb/225g raisins
2lb/900g granulated white sugar
1tsp/5g yeast nutrient
1tsp/5g grape tannin
All purpose wine yeast

Activate the yeast in a starter bottle. Boil the sugar in 1 pint/568 ml of water, and leave to cool. **(1)** Chop the raisins and place them in the fermenting bucket. **(2)** Bring the barley to the boil in 1 pint/0.5 litre of water, simmer for half an hour, and strain through a sieve onto the raisins. Leave to cool.

Remove the zest from the orange and lemon and add it to the bucket with the juice of the fruit. Add the cooled sugar syrup, the remainder of the ingredients and the yeast culture. Then add 3 pints/ 1.5 litres of cooled, boiled water; cover, and place in a warm position for five days, stirring the must daily. **(3)** Strain off the solids, putting the liquid into a sterile demijohn, top up to the shoulder as necessary, **(4)** and fit an airlock. Leave to ferment, shaking the jar daily. When fermentation has ended, remove the jar to a cool place and wait until a sediment has formed. Rack off in the usual way, add a crushed Campden tablet, and store until ready.

NOTE: this wine, made with ordinary barley, is not to be confused with the strong beer that is also known as Barley Wine; the latter is made with malted barley and hops.

❑ *Be careful not to include any of the pith of the citrus fruit, or the wine could have a bitterness to it.*

1

2

3

4

Amontillado Sherry Style

Medium Sweet Golden Social Wine

1lb/450g sultanas

1pt/0.5ltr white grape concentrate

2lb/1.1kg granulated white sugar

½tsp/3g citric acid

1tsp/5g yeast nutrient

Sherry style yeast

Activate the yeast in a starter bottle. Convert the sugar to a syrup by dissolving it in 1 pint/0.5 litre of boiling water. **(1)** Wash and rough dry, then **(2)** mince or chop the sultanas **(3)** and pour 4 pints/2.25 litres of boiling water over them. Add the sugar syrup.

(4) Leave to cool to 20°C (70°F), then add the grape concentrate, **(5)** additives and the **(6)** yeast culture. Cover and leave to ferment for six days, stirring daily to break up the sultana cap. **(7)** Strain through a sieve or cloth into a sterile 1 gallon/4.5 litre jar, **(8)** and top up to the shoulder with cool, boiled water. **(9)** Fit an airlock and leave in a warm place to ferment out, shaking the jar daily. When bubbles cease to escape from the airlock, move the jar to a cooler place and leave for the wine to clear and settle. Rack off as and when a sediment forms. Add a crushed Campden tablet and top up again with water or apple juice.

❏ *This wine should be a medium sweet wine, and can be sweetened up if necessary, preferably with a non-fermenting sweetener. This is another wine which can benefit from slight oxidation, and the jar can be plugged with cotton wool to achieve this.*

1

2

3

5

6

7

8

4

9

Mulls, punches, and cups

In the winter thoughts inevitably turn to the long, dark evenings, the colder weather, and Christmas, and perhaps we concentrate more on drinking our wines than on making them. The idyllic days of picnics and chilled apple wine have passed for another year, but what's wrong with toasted muffins and mulled wine? Here we have the perfect excuse to dispose of any wines that have not turned out quite as well as we had hoped. Yes, everybody makes them at some time! But when these wines are blended with cinnamon, ginger, or other spices, the slight imbalance they may have becomes less noticeable. Instead of asking the neighbours to come round to a barbecue, why not invite them to a punch party? A few of the author's ideas are outlined in this section, but really punch can be made from almost any ingredients you have to hand. However, can I put in one word of caution? If friends are coming from afar, be careful with the amount of spirits used as punch is very easy to drink, and a driver can quite easily go over the limit.

Mulled Wine

2pts/1ltr red wine

Grated rind and juice of a lemon and an orange

Brown sugar to taste

---

12 cloves stuck into three small oranges.

---

2 small sticks of cinnamon

---

(1) Place ingredients, except sugar, into a large saucepan and bring to the boil. Simmer for five minutes. **(2)** Strain into a punch bowl and add the sugar to taste, stirring continuously. Serve hot. If you like this and wish to use it for a special occasion, you can add ½ pint/280 ml of brandy to it. It does give it quite a lift!

1

Hot Coffee Rum

serves six

This is an excellent after-dinner drink, for which, if possible, the coffee should be freshly made from freshly-ground beans. **(1)** Into a small saucepan put six lumps of sugar, the finely pared rind (zest) of two oranges, six cloves, and a stick of cinnamon. Add enough rum to cover the sugar, and bring nearly to the boil, stirring gently until the sugar is dissolved. Take care that it does not catch fire. **(2)** When ready stir the mixture into six cups of very strong, very hot, black coffee and serve immediately. The perfect end to an evening, but your guests may not want to leave after tasting it.

1

2

Tea Punch

---

2 bottles of white wine

¼ bottle (17 cl) brandy

½pt/280ml sugar syrup (½lb225g sugar dissolved in ¼pt/140ml water)

2pts/1ltr strong tea

---

1 large lemon

Heat the wine, syrup, and juice of the lemon. Remove from the heat and add the brandy, slowly stir in the hot tea, and serve with slices of lemon. This is a perfect opportunity to use up any not-quite-perfect wines in the cellar.

Huntsman's Cup

1 bottle red wine
1 small glass cherry brandy (2fl oz/60ml)
1 glass brandy (4fl oz/120ml)
1 glass vodka (ditto)
¼pt/140ml sugar syrup (4oz/120g sugar dissolved in 2fl oz/60ml water)
2oz/60g honey (optional)
Cinnamon and nutmeg to taste

½ pint/280ml boiling water
1 sliced lemon

Heat the wine, honey, lemon, spices and syrup until very hot, but not boiling. Remove from the heat, then add the spirits and lastly the boiling water. Serve immediately.

❑ **As the name implies, this was served by landlords as a warming tot before the hunt.**

1

Bishop's Wassail

1 bottle red wine
1pt/0.5ltr water
½lb/225g honey
1 lemon and 1 orange, thinly sliced
4 cloves
1tsp/5g cinnamon

(1) Heat all the ingredients, stirring constantly, to just below boiling point. **(2)** Pour into a punch bowl. At this point you can add spirit and some raisins. If you add a generous amount of brandy it is possible to set a flame to it as a seasonal spectacle.

❏ *An ideal way to get a Christmas party off the ground, or to sup while at home in front of the fire.*

2

And just to show summer isn't quite forgotten, here is a recipe for

Chilled Summer Fruit Cup

2 bottles light white wine

2 bottles sparkling wine

¼ bottle gin (17 cl) (optional)

Sliced fruit (whatever you choose, but fresh summer fruits are nice)

Mix all the liquids together, sweeten to taste with sugar syrup, add the fruit and chill. Serve with ice. What nicer drink could be shared with friends on a warm summer's evening?

Liqueurs

One other type of drink that comes to mind for Christmas is the liqueur, and here we are quite able, with the help of extracts and flavourings, to imitate and reproduce many of the classic commercial liqueurs. There are two different ways of making a liqueur at home.

The first consists of allowing the fruit, with added sugar, to soak in the spirit until it has absorbed all the colour and flavour it can. In some cases the fruit will disintegrate and need to be strained out carefully.

A typical example of this method is sloe gin. To make this half fill a screw-top container with sloes, pricked at both ends to release the juice, add four to six ounces of sugar according to taste and the size of the jar, and top it up with gin. Seal the container and shake it vigorously. Continue to shake twice a day for two weeks, and then leave it to mature. This can be drunk after a few weeks, but improves if left for a year or more.

Distillation at home is illegal in this country, so the second method of making a liqueur involves using flavourings, which can be bought in home-brew shops. To make a liqueur you will need sugar syrup (a stock solution of 2 pounds/900 grams

of sugar brought to the boil in 1 pint/0.5 litre of water, and cooled), some spirit – Polish spirit is very good, if you can find it – some home-made wine, and a flavouring or extract. Often the flavouring comes complete with a recipe, but you can always use your own. Blend in small amounts at first, as adjustments are easy to make, but do keep a careful record, as it is even easier to forget after a few sample tastings. Unlike punches, poorer wines should not be used for liqueurs as the flavours are delicate; a good, clean wine is advisable.

The recipes in this section will act as a guide.

MATURING UNNECESSARY

Liqueurs are ready for drinking as soon as the flavours have had the opportunity to marry together, so there is no maturation time as such. The maturation processes, so important in winemaking, do not contribute to the flavour here, which comes almost entirely from the flavouring or extract. Even after being thoroughly shaken the ingredients will not have become completely mixed, partly because of the differing viscosities of the liquids

employed. Whilst the initial effect is more than adequate for blending and tasting purposes, it is better to prepare liqueurs at least two or three days before they are required.

As liqueurs are so high in alcohol, oxygen has far less effect on them than it has on wines. You can store liqueurs for long periods under air without deterioration, so do not worry if you have half-empty liqueur bottles in your drinks cabinet. This ease of storage allows you to build up a selection of the most luxurious of drinks, that can be enjoyed at the end of a dinner party, or sipped to round off that quiet evening at home. The various brands of flavourings and extracts should be available from your usual home-brew supplier.

❏ **With all the liqueur recipes, have fun blending and tasting at intervals, but beware of their high alcohol content.**

Egg Flip

The yolks of 3 large eggs
4fl oz/100ml sugar syrup
6fl oz/150ml gin or brandy
Vanilla essence to taste
Evaporated milk as required

Chill all the ingredients in the refrigerator. Beat the egg yolks well, and then add the sugar syrup, gin or brandy, and a little of the evaporated milk, say 4 fl oz/100ml. Continue beating until well blended. The ideal consistency of this liqueur is that it should only just pour, and only enough evaporated milk should be beaten in to achieve this consistency. The amount required largely depends on the size of the eggs used. Finally, add the vanilla essence to taste.

This will not keep indefinitely once made; always store in the refrigerator.

Creme de Menthe

4fl oz/100ml 80% spirit, or
8fl oz/200ml vodka

5fl oz/125ml sugar syrup

Creme de menthe essence as directed

Strong white table wine, such as
gooseberry, grape, or apple.

Experiment to find the blend that you
like best, following the above guidance.
Serve over crushed ice to make a frappé.

Cherry Brandy

3fl oz/75ml 80% Polish spirit (if
commercial spirits such as 37%
vodka are used, double this amount)

5fl oz/125ml sugar syrup (ie,
2lbs/900g sugar dissolved in
1pt/0.5ltr water)

Cherry brandy essence/flavouring:
use as directed on the bottle

A strong red wine, such as cherry,
elderberry, or bilberry

Blend the spirit, wine, and syrup in the
proportions of 3:7:2, add the essence as
recommended, and taste. Adjust to suit
yourself, and bottle. Using an eye
dropper or even a teaspoon will give you
ample scope for adjustments, but be sure
you keep a note of them as you go along,
otherwise you won't be able to scale up
your experiments. The above proportions
as fluid ounces will give almost a half-
bottle of liqueur.

Making Wine from Grapes

1

5

2

3

4

6

Red wine to make 1 Gallon

12-13lbs/5.5-6kg red grapes

Burgundy or general purpose wine yeast

Campden tablets

Tartaric acid

Sugar

English outdoor-grown red grapes usually contain higher levels of acidity than imported ones due to the relatively short ripening period. To reduce the acidity use precipitated chalk (calcium carbonate).

If only dessert grapes are available, add a ½ teaspoon of tartaric acid – this will raise the acid level, improving the balance and taste.

(1) Pick and remove the grapes from the stalk and place in a clean, sterilized fermentation bucket. **(2)** Add a crushed Campden tablet and **(3)** crush the grapes. Strain off some of the juice and check the S.G., which should be 1,090 to give 12 percent by volume of alcohol in the finished wine. Add sugar if required to raise the S.G. **(4)** Add the yeast starter to the pulp and leave to ferment.

Stir often to keep the pulp submerged within the juice to extract the red pigmentation and tannin from the skins. If you are making rosé wine you need only ferment for a short period, 8-10 hours, to extract sufficient colouring, otherwise leave on the pulp for 7-9 days.

(5) Press the pulp and strain the 'must' into a clean, sterilized demijohn – if necessary top up with cooled boiled water.

(6) Place the demijohn in a warm room 50-60°F/10-15°C and allow the fermentation to complete. Rack off after completion.

Rack every 10-12 weeks and add a crushed Campden tablet after each racking. Top up with a similar wine or cooled boiled water.

Bottle when the wine is crystal clear and stable; leave to mature. This wine is best drunk after a year.

White wine to make 1 Gallon

To make 1 Gallon/4.5 litres

12-13lbs/5.5-6kg white grapes
Hock or general purpose wine yeast
Tartaric acid
Campden tablet
Sugar

Sterilize all equipment. If you are able to obtain wine grapes, go straight to the crushing stage. Dessert grapes require the addition of a ½ teaspoon of tartaric acid to the must.

(1) Before crushing, remove the stalks and **(2)** sprinkle a crushed Campden tablet onto the grapes. **(3)** Press the grapes and leave to stand for an hour; this will allow the natural enzymes within the grape to break down the pulp and will aid extraction of the juice.

(4) Pour the pulp into the wine press, extract the juice, strain into a demijohn and allow to stand overnight to enable the minute pulp particles to settle. **(5)** Rack the cleared juice into a clean, sterilized demijohn.

Check the sugar content with a hydrometer; the juice should have a minimum S.G. of 1.075 to produce a table wine with 10 percent by volume of alcohol. Add sugar if required.

(6) Add the yeast previously prepared in a starter bottle, place the demijohn in a warm room 50-60°F/10-15°C and allow to ferment. Fermentation will slow after 2-3 weeks and the wine will begin to clear.

After the fermentation has finished, rack into a clean demijohn, then, if necessary, top up with a similar wine or

cooled boiled water and add a Campden tablet.

(7) Leave to mature, racking every 10-12 weeks and adding a crushed Campden tablet after each racking until the wine is crystal clear and stable. White wine is best drunk young and bottled in the spring following the vintage. With practise, wines mage from grapes in this way can rival commercially produced wines.

1

2

3

4

5

6

7

Trophy-winning Wines

Throughout the country, wine is being made by people who enjoy making a worthwhile alcoholic drink. Different people make wine for different reasons: some like to make quick kit wines that they can drink at once; some make out-of-the-ordinary wines like pea-pod. The majority make wines to drink socially with their friends, but some have a real attempt at making wines for competition, and hope to win with them. Competitions are at several different levels – the circle, the regional federation, the local horticultural shows, and the national. At the really big shows, some of which attract nearly 5,000 bottles in a variety of classes, the only real chance you have of winning a first prize is to set out at the very beginning to make a prize-winning wine! Such wines do not just happen!

We know, of course, that the wine we buy is made from grapes – in fact, the definition of wine is 'liquor produced from freshly-expressed grape juice by natural fermentation'. The grapes that we are able to grow outdoors in England, and that really only in the southern half of the country, can be made into wine, but there is a large amount of work and good luck in doing so successfully. The grapes that make the best wine come from abroad, where there is an abundance of sunshine. It is not easy to buy imported wine grapes here, but some groups of winemakers club together to do just that. Several people in an area may jointly order a substantial quantity of grapes, and one member takes a vehicle to collect them. For instance, in a recent year members of the Tyneside club brought over three tons of Italian winemaking grapes. The imported grapes can then be shared out, and the work begins. A grape crusher is hired, and set up in one person's premises; his share of the fruit is washed in a weak sulphite solution, and the berries stripped from the bunches. The fruit is crushed, and the juice collected. All the family can take part, and as soon as one winemaker finishes with the press it is transported to the next person. The wine is then made, as commercially, with pure grape juice and the addition of sugar if necessary.

If white wine is to be made, the juice is immediately separated from the skins. The juice of all grapes is white, even from black varieties; Champagne is actually made from a blend of black Pinot grapes and white Chardonnay grapes while Blanc de Noirs Champagne is actually made just from the Pinot Noir grape, a dark red variety. If a red wine is required, the juice is kept with the pulp for three to four days to extract the colour from the skins. The longer they are kept together, the the darker the wine will be. But at the same time as colour is extracted, so is tannin. If the tannin content is too high, the wine will take longer to mature. In any event, this type of wine will not be at its best for four years at least. Not everyone wants to go to the trouble of buying and crushing grapes to make fine wines. It is possible to do this from the fruits around us. As already mentioned earlier in this book, the end product can only reflect the ingredients used. From this it is easy to see that to make prize-winning wines you must use good, clean and ripe fruit. To obtain the body required you must have plenty of the ingredients, and to produce the

correct level of alcohol the right temperature, and a constant temperature to keep the fermentation going. The one overall point to remember is that a wine judge is looking for a well-balanced, well-made wine, which has all the correct characteristics for the style of wine asked for.

Do be very careful to read your schedule before entering a show. The classes will be clearly defined. The colour is always stated, red, white, rosé, golden, any colour, etc. The sweetness level is nearly always printed – dry, medium dry, sweet and so on. Also the style of wine is mentioned, such as table, social, aperitif. Many people lose points simply because they do not read the whole definition.

The other very important aspect to remember is the presentation of the bottle. The rules for this will be included in the schedule. The size, shape, and colour of the bottle, and the colour and type of stopper are important: use the wrong ones and you lose points. Points can be lost for the label – the rules will tell you where it should be affixed – usually between the bottle seams and a specified distance from the base of the bottle. Many shows provide the standard bottle you must use. These points are all important, though to the onlooker they may seem pedantic. The reason for them is that if all the rules are followed the bottles will be identical, and the judge cannot pick out any one individual's wine. Justice has to be seen to be done.

Below are a few selected recipes for wines that have won in major competitions, but the possible choice is unlimited. By trial and experimentation you can adapt your own favourite recipes. Remember, because of the extra body and careful balance, these wines will almost certainly need some time to mature and become potential prize-winning entries.

TROPHY-WINNING RECIPES

By now, if you have worked your way through this book, you should be making very presentable wines. Hopefully, you have also joined a club or association, and are enjoying the pleasure of sharing your wine with others. If this is the case, I would expect you to be interested now in entering shows and competitions, and nothing is more rewarding than to win first place and to be presented with a trophy. Generally, your name and the year in which you won the award are engraved on the cup, and so the record of your achievement is preserved for posterity.

All classes, whatever their standard, are assessed by a judge, and it is very useful to know just what that judge will be looking for. First and foremost he will look at the appearance of the entry. Are both bottle and cork clean and of the correct type? Is there a sediment on the bottom of the bottle, or a haze in the wine? Is the label on straight and in the correct position? These details can always be found in the show Schedule. Is the colour correct? This point is very important; if the class description states 'White to Golden' it does not mean dark tawny, and if the schedule says 'Red' it does not mean rosé. Indeed, in the case of rosé wines the colour is very important. It can vary from very pale pink to a deeper shade, but it must not have any signs of brown or deep red in it.

Secondly, the judge will assess the bouquet. Is it clean and fresh, does it appeal, is it suitable for the style of wine presented? An excellent example of this is with flower wines, these should have a characteristic bouquet of the ingredient used; if they do not they lose marks. If the entry is a white table wine, the bouquet should not be so strong as to overpower the food it is served with.

The contents of the bottle is, of course, the most important element, and this will be judged on balance, flavour, appeal and how it represents the class it has been entered in. If the class is for dry wines no recognisable sweetness is

Dry White Table Wine

To make 1 gallon/4.5 litres:

3lb/1.36kg green gooseberries

1lb/450g green apples

1pt/500ml white grape concentrate

2lb/900g granulated white sugar

1tsp/5g tartaric acid

1tsp/5g tannin

1tsp/5g yeast nutrient

1tsp/5g pectic enzyme

1 x 3 mg vitamin B tablet

1 packet of Chablis type yeast

Activate the yeast by adding to it a cup of lukewarm water, shake or stir well, cover, and leave in the warm. Wash the fruit, top and tail the gooseberries, and place them in the fermentation bucket. Grate the apples, including the skins and cores, onto the gooseberries. Dissolve the sugar in 1 pint/568 ml of boiling water, and pour it over the fruit. Add a further 4½ pints/2.5 litres of boiling water.

(1) When the water in the bucket has cooled down, break down the fruit, either with a masher or by hand, making sure that all the skins of the gooseberries are broken. Add the grape concentrate, acid, enzyme, nutrients and tannin, and the activated yeast. Stir well, cover, and leave in a warm place to ferment for four days, stirring at least once daily.

(2) Fit an airlock and leave in the warm until fermentation has ceased. It is advisable to shake the jar daily. When the wine has completed its fermentation, move it to a cool place and allow it to settle.

It is very important that you do not allow this wine to sit on the lees, or sediment, for any length of time. If this does happen the wine will be spoilt by an off-flavour of yeast. You must therefore rack regularly, whenever a sediment forms. One crushed Campden tablet is added at the first racking after fermentation ends, but not thereafter. After the initial frothy fermentation has died down the demijohn should be kept topped up to the neck to avoid oxidation. This can be done with cooled, boiled water or apple juice; the latter has the advantage of not weakening the wine.

When the wine is finally clear add one more Campden tablet and seal the jar. Leave in a cool place to mature. To obtain a really crystal-clear wine you can use finings or a filter. Both are described in a previous chapter. This wine needs at least one year to reach full maturity.

1

2

permitted. If the competitor is asked for a dessert-style wine, the assessor would expect a sweet, full-bodied, high alcohol wine with plenty of flavour. If, however, the class is dry table wine it would be expected to be lower in alcohol, slight in flavour and with no sweetness.

All wines are judged on a points system: the person responsible awards marks out of the permitted total for each section and these are totalled at the end. National judges work on the following guide lines:

Presentation 2. Clarity 4. Colour 4. Bouquet 10. Taste 30. Making a total of 50 points.

There is then a final judge-off between the wines that have scored the highest marks, to ascertain the final placings.

There is a small paperback book called *Judging Wine & Beer*, published by the National Guild of Judges, which explains in detail all the above mentioned points. Although this is really meant as an informative guide to judges and stewards, it is also of tremendous help to the competitors.

Below are listed several recipes which have won prizes at different shows, but the art of really successful winemaking is in adapting a recipe to your own liking. This can be great fun, but do write down everything you do and use. Nothing is more frustrating than to make a really first class, award-winning wine, and then being unable to remember the details and therefore unable to repeat it.

Red Dessert Wine

To make 1 gallon/4.5 litres:

3lb/1.36kg elderberries
2lb/900g blackberries
1lb/450g sloes
1lb/450g sultanas
1pt/500ml red grape concentrate
1lb/450g overripe bananas
½lb/225g dried rose hip shells
3lb/1.36kg granulated white sugar (at least)
1tsp/5g tartaric acid
1tsp/5g yeast nutrient
1tsp/5g pectic enzyme
1 x 3 mg vitamin B tablet
1 packet of Port or Tokay type yeast

Activate the yeast in a cupful of warm water, cover, and leave in a warm place. Wash all the fruit in a sulphite solution (one Campden tablet per pint). Separate the elderberries from their stalks. **(1)** Stone the sloes. Chop the sultanas, making sure every one is broken. Peel and cut the bananas into small chunks, and bring them to the boil in 2 pints/1.2 litres of water, then simmer for another twenty minutes. Soak the rosehips in 1 pint/0.5 litre of boiling water. Dissolve 2 pounds/900 grams of the sugar in 1 pint/0.5 litre of boiling water.

Place all the fruit in a sterilised white plastic bucket of two gallons capacity. **(2)** Strain the banana liquor into the bucket, and discard the banana pulp. Add the rose hips together together with the water they were soaked in. Tip on the boiling sugar syrup. Add a further 1 pint/ 0.5 litre boiling water, stir well, and cover and leave to cool to blood heat. **(3)** When cool add the grape concentrate and the other additives and stir well. Add the yeast culture, cover, and leave in a warm place to start fermenting. This should soon become vigorous, and a 'cap' of fruit will form on top of the must. This should be stirred in at least twice a

1

2

3

day, to extract the maximum goodness from the fruit.

After five days strain the must through a sieve or cloth, and place the juice into a sterilised demijohn. Do not squeeze the pulp to get the last drops from it, as this will force fine particles of pulp through the straining cloth, and it will form too heavy a sediment. If necessary, top up the jar to just below the shoulder, but leave room for more sugar syrup. Convert another 1 pound/450 grams of sugar to syrup in ½ pint/284 ml of boiling water. Cool, and keep this to one side in a stoppered bottle for use in the next few days. Fit an airlock, and replace the demijohn in the warm area and leave it for three days, shaking the jar daily.

(4) Pour some of the wine into a trial jar or other tall vessel, and read the specific gravity from a hydrometer. If it has dropped to 1025 or less, add 4 fluid ounces/100 ml of sugar syrup. Repeat this test every second day, adding syrup when the gravity drops below 1025, until the fermentation slows right down. It may be necessary to make more syrup. When no further additions are being made, leave the jar for the fermentation to finish slowly and for the yeast to begin to settle.

Rack the wine into a clean jar, and top up to the neck with a little red grape juice. Add a crushed Campden tablet to help stabilise the wine. Repeat the racking when necessary, but do not add any more Campden tablets, until the wine is perfectly clear.

Because this wine was left on the pulp to ferment at the beginning, it will take some time for the tannins and acids to balance out and mellow. The wine will probably be at its best in anything from two and a half to four years. Store it, well stoppered, in a cool place, and check it regularly.

4

Fino sherry style

To make 1 gallon/4.5 litres:

1lb/450g parsnips
1lb/450g carrots
1lb/450g sultanas
2pts/1.2ltr pure apple juice
2lb/900g granulated white sugar
1tsp/5g tartaric acid
1tsp/5g yeast nutrient
1tsp/5g pectic enzyme
1 packet of Sherry yeast

Activate the yeast in a little warm water, and put aside. Scrub the vegetables, chop them, and boil them in 4 pints/2.25 litres of water for ten to fifteen minutes, or until soft but not mushy. Chop the sultanas. Convert the sugar to syrup by bringing it to the boil in 1 pint/568 ml of water.

Place the sultanas in a fermentation bucket, strain over them the liquid from the vegetables, discarding the carrot and parsnip solids **(1)**, or saving them to freeze and eat at a later date. Add the sugar syrup. Leave to cool, then add the apple juice **(2)**. Next stir in the pectic enzyme, acid, yeast nutrient and yeast culture **(3)**. Cover **(4)** and leave in a warm place to begin fermentation. Stir daily – it is advisable to hand crush the sultanas after two or three days to ensure they are well broken down. After five days strain off the must from the solids.

Place the must in a demijohn, top up to the shoulder with more apple juice, fit an airlock and return the jar to the warmth. Shake daily until the fermentation finishes. If a high alcohol level is desired, add more syrup as described in the Red Dessert recipe, in 2 fluid ounce/50 ml amounts each time the SG drops to 1000. When the fermentation is complete, remove the demijohn to a cool place and allow the yeast to settle. At this point replace the airlock with a wad of unmedicated cotton-wool, as a small amount of oxidation improves the sherry characteristics of this wine. Rack as with the other recipes until the wine is bright and clear. It is not advisable to leave the wine without an airtight bung for more than three months.

1

2

3

4

Oloroso Sherry Style

To make 1 gallon/4.5 litres:

1lb/450g figs
1lb/450g sultanas
1lb/450g bananas (over ripe if possible, not green)
1lb/450g dried apricots
2lb/900g soft brown sugar
1tsp/5g citric acid
1tsp/5g yeast nutrient
1tsp/5g pectic enzyme
1 Sherry yeast

Start the yeast working by adding it to a small amount of warm water. Skin the bananas, chop them into small pieces, and place in 3 pints/1.7 litres of water and boil for thirty minutes. Rinse the dried fruit in warm water to remove any preservatives, rough dry it with a cloth, and chop it up. Place it in a sterilised fermentation bucket. Turn the sugar into a syrup by stirring it into 1 pint/568 ml of boiling water.

Strain the 'gravy' **(1)** from the bananas over the chopped fruit, add the syrup and 2 pints/1.14 litres of boiling water, and stir thoroughly. Cover **(2)**, leave to cool, then put in the additives and yeast culture and stir again. Re-cover and leave in a warm place to ferment. From this point, proceed as for the Fino Sherry, but add more sugar to the finished wine for a sweeter product.

1

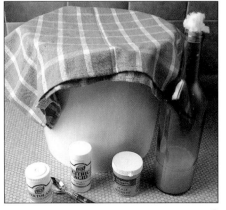

2

Medium Dry Rosé Wine

To make 1 gallon/4.5 litres:

4lb/1.8kg rhubarb

½ pint/280ml red grape concentrate

2lb/900g granulated white sugar

½ tsp/3g tartaric acid

1tsp/5g yeast nutrient

1tsp/5g pectic enzyme

1 x 3 mg vitamin B tablet

1 sachet of table wine yeast

1

Rhubarb has a very high natural acid content, and if it comes into contact with hot water this acid is extracted. It is therefore advantageous to use a cold water method of extraction. To assist this, it is advisable to pre- reeze the fruit before use, as this helps break down the cell walls more easily. Wash the stalks clean with a mild solution of sulphite (1 Campden tablet per 1 pint/0.5 litre of water) and chop them into 2-3 inch/5-8 cm lengths **(1)**. Place these in polythene containers or bags **(2)**, and let them freeze for at least forty eight hours. Do not put them in the fast-freeze section, slow freezing is better for juice extraction later. The rhubarb can be kept in the freezer for use at any time in the year.

Activate the yeast in a small amount of warm water. Place the frozen rhubarb in a bucket and allow to thaw for twenty-four hours. Pour over it 4 pints/2.25 litres of lukewarm water. Turn the sugar into syrup with 1 pint/0.5 litre of boiling water, and leave to cool, then pour it into the bucket. Add the grape concentrate **(3)** and the additives, and stir well. Cover, and leave in a warm place.

After twelve hours crush the fruit by hand **(4)** and add the activated yeast. Cover and return to a warm place for fermentation to begin. Stir daily for three days.

Strain the must through a sieve – it is not advisable to squeeze the solids. Transfer the must to a demijohn, and top up to the shoulder with cool, boiled water. Fit an airlock and leave in a warm place until fermentation has ceased.

Move the demijohn to a cool place and

2

wait until a sediment has formed. Rack the young wine into a clean jar, top up, and add a crushed Campden tablet. Refit the airlock, and replace the jar in the cool. Rack again as necessary, but only adding one more Campden tablet, and that at the final racking.

It may be necessary to sweeten this wine at the end to produce the medium dry finish that is expected of a rosé. To do this, and to ensure that there will not be any secondary fermentation, try using a non-fermentable sweetener. These are easily available in homebrew and health food shops. A word of warning: use very sparingly to begin with, as these are very concentrated sweeteners. Remember, you can always add a little more, but you can never take it out once it is there.

This wine should be drinkable within twelve months.

3

4

Medium Dry White Table Wine

To make 1 gallon/4.5 litres:

6pts/3ltr preservative-free pure apple juice

3 heads of fresh elderflower, or 1oz/ 30g of dried elderflower.

1½lb/675g granulated white sugar

1tsp/5g tartaric acid

1tsp/5g yeast nutrient

1tsp/5g pectic enzyme

1 x 3mg vitamin B tablet

1 packet of German-style yeast

Activate the yeast with a little warm water. **(1)** Pour the apple juice into a bucket, and add the sugar (converted to a syrup with 1 pint/0.5 litre of boiling water and added whilst still hot). Wash the fresh elderflower, trim any excess stalks away, and add it to the bucket **(2)**. Dried flowers can be added straight to the bucket. When cool, add the acid, nutrients, and pectic enzyme. Stir well, and pour in the yeast. Cover and leave in a warm place for fermentation to begin. Stir daily for three days, then strain the must into a demijohn **(3)** and proceed in the normal way. Rack, top up and add a crushed Campden tablet when the wine clears, and then store. This wine can be ready to drink in three months, but will improve if kept for six months.

❑ *This is a very easy and quick way of producing drinkable German-style table wine. The main point to watch is the quality of the apple juice. As stated before, the end product is subject to the ingredients, and it is well worth purchasing good quality juice, which has not been treated in any way or reconstituted from concentrates.*

1

2

3

POISONOUS OR UNSUITABLE PLANTS

This list is a general guide to common plants, and is not exhaustive.

Anemones (Pasque Flowers)
Arum Lilies (Lords & Ladies, Cuckoo Pint)
Azaleas
Bane – any plant with 'bane' in its name. Bane is an old word for poison
Bryonies, both Black and White
Buckthorns, both Alder and Common (Purging)
Bulbs, such as Daffodils, Tulips, Lilies, Crocus etc., or their flowers.
Buttercup family (Marsh Marigold, Celandine, Yellow Wood Anemone etc.)
Cabbage Family – Cruciferæ (Brussels, Cauliflowers, Spring Greens etc.)
Christmas Rose (Hellebores)
Columbine (Aquilegia)
Cow Parsley. There are many plants that go under this name to the non-botanist, and several are poisonous. They have long tubular stalks, and a flat umbrella of white or whitish flowers on top. It is recommended that you ignore all this group, except Sweet Cicely, which smells strongly of aniseed.
Clematis (Traveller's Joy and garden varieties)
Dwarf Elder (Danewort)
Ferns
Foxglove
Fungi: Mushrooms are safe, but a poor ingredient. Other fungi are decidedly risky and some are swiftly lethal!

Geranium, Cranesbill, Pelargonium
Groundsel, Ragwort, Fleawort etc.
Hemlock
Honeysuckle, all except flowers
Iris (Flag) family
Ivies
Laburnum
Laurel, Cherry or Portuguese
Lilac
Lobelias
Lupins
Meadow Rue, Common
Meadow Saffron
Mercury, Annual and Dog's
Mistletoe
Monkshood
Nightshades (Black or Garden, Deadly, or Woody [Bittersweet])
Pæony
Poppies, various
Potatoes, except for green-free tubers
Privets, (Garden-Hedge, Oval-Leaved, or the British native privet)
Rhododendron
Rhubarb, except stalks
Soapwort
Spindle Tree
Pea, (Broad Leaved Everlasting, Sweet Pea)
Thornapple or Jimson Weed – *Datura stramonium*. In the USA, Thornapple is often the name for Hawthorns, *Cratægus* spp., which are harmless
Tomatoes, except for fruit
Yews, Common or Irish.

Azalea

Daffodil

Laburnum

Pæony

Anemone

Celandine

Christmas Rose

Clematis

Foxglove

Geranium

Iris

Laurel

Lilac

Mistletoe

Poppy

Rhododendron

Soapwort

Index

O

Oloroso Sherry Style Wine 147
Orange and Apple Wine 51
Orange and Banana Wine 69
Orange Blossom and Grape Concentrate
   Wine 38

P

Parsley Wine 42
Parsnip Wine 115
Pea Pod Wine 68
Plum or Apricot Wine 76
Potato Wine 110
Prune Wine 102

R

Red Dessert Wine 144
Red Wine from Grapes 137
Ribena or Blackcurrant Wine 55

Rice and Raisin Wine 98
Rose Petal and Grape Concentrate
   Wine 78
Rosehip Wine 96
Royal Elderberry Wine 87

S

Seville Orange Wine 52
Sloe Gin 88
Sloe, Sultana and Grape Juice Wine 90
Strawberry Wine 63
Sweet Basil and Rosehip Wine 40
Royal Elderberry Wine 87

T

Tea Wine 49
Tea Punch 129

V

Vine Pruning 'Folly' 65

W

Wheat and Raisin Wine 99
Wheat Whiskey 100
White Wine from Grapes 138